SCC Library

3 3065 00348 7448

D0744814

Philosophical Dialectics

B
53
. R432
2006

Philosophical Dialectics

An Essay on Metaphilosophy

Nicholas Rescher

State University of New York Press

OCM 60515276

Santiago Canyon College
Library

Published by
State University of New York Press, Albany

© 2006 State University of New York

All rights reserved

Printed in the United States of America

No part of this book may be used or reproduced in any manner whatsoever
without written permission. No part of this book may be stored in a retrieval system
or transmitted in any form or by any means including electronic, electrostatic,
magnetic tape, mechanical, photocopying, recording, or otherwise
without the prior permission in writing of the publisher.

For information, address State University of New York Press,
194 Washington Avenue, Suite 305, Albany, NY 12210-2384

Production by Marilyn P. Semerad
Marketing by Anne M. Valentine

Library of Congress Cataloging-in Publication Data

Rescher, Nicholas.
  Philosophical dialectics : an essay on metaphilosophy / Nicholas Rescher.
     p.cm.
  Includes bibliographical references and index.
  ISBN-13: 978-0-7914-6745-9 (hardcover : alk. paper)
  ISBN-10: 0-7914-6745-7 (hardcover : alk. paper)
  ISBN-13: 978-0-7914-6746-6 (pbk : alk. paper)

  1. Methodology.   2. Philosophy.   3. Metaphysics.   4. Process philosophy.
5. Dialectic.   I. Title.
B53.R432 2006
101—dc22
                                                          2005014630

10 9 8 7 6 5 4 3 2 1

Contents

Preface   vii

1. Philosophical Principles   1
   Philosophical Principles 1 ❧ Principles of Informative
   Adequacy 3 ❧ Probative Principles of Rational Cogency 5 ❧
   Principles of Rational Economy 7 ❧ Issues of Validation 10 ❧
   Dealing with Objections 14

2. Aporetic Method in Philosophy   17
   Consistency and Apories 17 ❧ Some Sample Apories 19 ❧
   On Appraising Apories 21 ❧ Enter Distinctions 23 ❧
   Apory Resolution as Cost-Benefit Analysis 24

3. On Distinctions in Philosophy   27
   What Distinctions Are 27 ❧ How Distinctions Fail 29 ❧
   Misassimilation 31 ❧ Historical Background 35 ❧ The Role
   of Distinctions in Philosophy 36 ❧ Philosophical Apories
   Tie Issues Together 41

4. Respect Neglect and Misassimilation as Fallacies of
   Philosophical Distinctions   45
   Respect Neglect 45 ❧ Simplicity 46 ❧ Fallacy 47

5. Systemic Interconnectedness and Explanatory Holism
   in Philosophy   51
   The Problem 51 ❧ Summative Features 52 ❧ Fallacies of
   Composition and Division 53 ❧ Is Existence Mereologically
   Summative? No—A Whole is More Than Its Parts 53 ❧

The Analytical/Constructionist Program 54 ❧ Instances of the Implementation of the Constructionist Program 55 ❧ Problem Number One: The Fallacy of Termination Presumption 60 ❧ Problem Number Two: The Disintegration of Simplicity and the Fallacy of Respect Neglect 61 ❧ Perspectival Dissonance and Nonamalgamation 62 ❧ Cognition Is Not Summative 63 ❧ Review 65 ❧ Externalities and Negative Side Effects 66 ❧ Systematic Interconnectedness as a Consequence of Aporetic Complexity 71

6. The Structure of Philosophical Dialectic   75
Philosophical Aporetics 75 ❧ The Role of Distinctions 78 ❧ The Structure of Dialectic 81 ❧ Developmental Dialectics 84 ❧ The Burden of History 89 ❧ The Structure of Philosophical History 92

7. Ignorance and Cognitive Horizons   95
Ignorance 95 ❧ Intractable Questions about the Cognitive Future and Surd Generalties 97 ❧ Insolubilia Then and Now 100 ❧ Cognitive Limits 102 ❧ Identifying Insolubilia 104 ❧ Relating Knowledge to Ignorance 106

Notes   109

Bibliography   115

Index   119

Preface

While the pursuit of the philosophy of various studies (of science, of art, of politics, etc.) has recently blossomed, the philosophy of philosophy remains a comparatively neglected domain. The present book offers a further small contribution toward filling a very large gap.

Overall, the book's argumentation proceeds by way of unfolding the following story line. Philosophy is a purposive venture with characteristic aims of its own whose pursuit leads the enterprise into certain particular methodological pathways (chapter 1). The course of problem resolution along these pathways makes for a dialectical development (chapter 2) that requires ever subtler and more sophisticated distinctions (chapter 3). In this regard respect neglect can prove a fatal error (chapter 6). Its systematic aspirations mean that the usual recourse to partitioning, specialization, and division of labor will not work in philosophy (chapter 5), with the result that as this discipline develops it becomes engaged in grappling with increasingly complex and intricate problem solving (chapter 6). And in the end this leads into an area of unanswerable questions and insolubilia—issues whose nature precludes our ever conclusively achieving the aims of the enterprise (chapter 7).

And so the book begins with a discussion of philosophical principles and methods, and then unfolds step by step a story of how philosophical inquiry faces the ever more formidable difficulties that arise in a complex and widely variegated world. Fortunately, however, this inability to resolve *all* the problems of the field nowise precludes the prospect of achieving a satisfactory resolution of many or even most of them.

On this basis, the present book presents not only a panorama of metaphilosophical issues but also a theory of metaphilosophy. For it takes the discipline to develop dialectically in a context of increasing complexity, detail, and subtlety of deliberation that moves the issues ever further in the direction of intractability and inscrutability. Although that aim of the enterprise is clarification, its net effect is to lead through this very process to an increasingly less manageable residue of problematic issues.

I am indebted to Estelle Burris for her excellent assistance in preparing this material for publication.

Nicholas Rescher

Pittsburgh PA
September 2004

Chapter 1

Philosophical Principles

Philosophical Principles

Metaphilosophy is the philosophical examination of the practice of philosophizing itself. Its definitive aim is to study the methods of the field in an endeavor to illuminate its promise and prospects. And in addressing the issues that arise here, there is no better place to begin than by considering the rules and principles of procedure that provide the guidelines for cultivating this historic realm of rational deliberation.

For Plato, principles were the root source (*archai*) of being or of knowledge.[1] For Aristotle, they were the "first cause" of being, of becoming, or of being known (*hothen hē estin hē gignetai hē gignōsketai*).[2] And much the same conception is at issue with Thomas Aquinas, for whom a principle (*principium*) was something primary in the being of a thing, or in its becoming, or in knowledge of it (*quod est primum aut in esse rei . . . aut in fieri rei, . . . aut in rei cognitione*).[3] As standard philosophical usage has evolved in the light of these ideas, a principle is viewed as something basic—as a *fundamentum* (Latin) or *archē* (Greek). In particular, a proposition that is a principle either admits no proof (is axiomatic) or does not need proof (is obvious and self-evident). Moreover, it must be abstract by way of applying to a broad range of cases. Thus, all concerned seem agreed that principles are fundamental generalities governing our understanding of the modus operandi of some knowledge-accessible domain.

Against this background, a specifically *philosophical principle*, in the sense of the term that is to be at issue here, is a general instruction for cogent philosophizing, a maxim that lays down a methodological rule for philosophical practice. It is not a philosophical thesis or doctrine that purports to answer to some substantive philosophical question. Instead, it is a rule of procedure that specifies a modus operandi, a way of proceeding in the course of philosophizing. A methodological principle of this sort is thus to philosophy what a maxim like "always keep your promises" is to morality. It represents a guideline to be followed if error is to be avoided. Such methodological principles are general rules of procedure, framed in terms of maxims that prescribe the appropriateness or inappropriateness of different ways of proceeding in philosophizing.[4] In matters of philosophy, after all, understanding clearly hinges not simply on the instruction of theses and doctrines, but on grasping the underlying principles within whose frame of reference such substantive dealings are articulated in the first place.

To be sure, *within* philosophy one also encounters a profusion of principles. In ethics, there is the "principle of utility," which holds that the rightness of an action lies in its capacity to conduce to the greatest good of the greatest number; in natural philosophy, we have the "principle of causality," which holds that every event has a cause; and in epistemology, we have the "principle of truth," which holds that only what is true can be said to be known to someone: $(\exists x)Kxp \rightarrow p$. But such principles are principles IN philosophy, not principles OF philosophy—that is, they are not procedural principles of philosophizing of the sort that concern us here.[5]

What argues for principles? What is their justifactory rationale? Clearly it is—or ought to be—the factor of functional efficacy. After all, philosophizing is a purposive enterprise. It has an aim or mission: to enable us to orient ourselves in thought and action, enabling us to get a clearer understanding of the big issues of our place and our prospects in a complex world that is not of our own making. And the validation of a philosophical principle must in the final analysis rest on its promise and performance in fostering this enterprise.

Will all philosophers agree with regard to principles? Of course not! After all, there is, it would seem, very little that *all* philosophers agree on.[6] All that can be said in this regard is (1) that what puts a principle on the agenda is the preaching—and, even more importantly, the practice—of prominent philosophers and (2) that when a philosopher explicitly espouses such a principle, he will generally offer (or at least *have*) plausible reasons for doing so. To be sure, difficulties sometimes arise. Thus, for example, the tendency of C. S. Peirce's sensible principle that the aim of rational inquiry is to settle opinion among intelligent interagents seems to be flaunted by the Socrates of Plato's writings, who often seeks to destabilize opinion in the initial stages of a dialogue to unsettle judgment into a condition of perplexity or aporia. The creation of a state of ignorance and uncertainty is thus seen as a desirable goal—in seeming conflict with various familiar philosophical principles. But of course Socratic practice makes it all too clear that this is only the starting point for an honest and open-minded inquiry, whose ultimate goal is to erect a new structure of understanding on the reviews of prior misconceptions.

Be this as it may, procedural principles are in the end validated through the consideration of this utility and efficacy on the particular domain at practice that is at issue. Basically they are of three kinds: principles of informative adequacy to facilitate understanding, principles of rational cogency to assure convincing argumentation, and principles of rational economy to avert needless labor in production and avoidable difficulty in consumption.

Principles of Informative Adequacy

The principles arising under this rubric address the problem of providing adequate information—of facilitating the business of understanding and enabling us to get a secure cognitive grip on the issues at hand.

#1

NEVER BAR THE PATH OF INQUIRY (C. S. Peirce). Peirce envisioned for this principle a correlative range of application that turns on the following line of thought: "Never adopt a methodological stance that would systematically prevent the discovery of something that could turn out to be true." What can and should prevent one's acceptance of a certain factual claim is the discovery of its falsity through the ascertainment of some other factual claim that is incompatible with it. But only facts should be able to block the route to the serious consideration of a factual thesis, and never purely methodological/procedural general principles.

For one thing, radical skepticism—"Never accept anything"—would fall immediate victim to this principle. For if we adopt this line of radical skepticism, all progress is blocked from the very outset. Again, if one systematically refused to give credence to reasoning by analogy, then any prospect of discovery of facts about other minds would be precluded: even if it were the case that other people have mental lives akin to our own, we could never warrant a belief in this circumstance if we could not somehow base on that which is claims about that which is inaccessible in our experience.

Or again, a Cartesian insistence on absolute certainty precludes any sense-based access whatsoever to information about the world's arrangements since sensory experience can never conclusively validate objective claims. (There is always an epistemic gap between the subjective phenomenology of how things appear to us and what features they actually and impersonally have.)

#2

ALL AFFIRMATION IS NEGATION: *omnis affirmatio est negatio* (Spinoza). A positive claim always stands correlative to a corresponding negative. To characterize something in some way or other is to contradistinguish it from that to which that characterization does not apply. There is no communicative point in ascribing a feature to something when this does not effectively separate and distinguish what this feature involves from what it excludes.

Now, for philosophy in specific this means that we can only clarify what a doctrine asserts and maintains if the same time we become clear about what it denies and rejects. Any thesis or position must make manifest its particular substance and purport in the setting of a contrast with the various rivals that contest the doctrinal ground at issue.

#3

NO ENTITY WITHOUT IDENTITY (W. V. Quine). This is a modern version of the medieval principle *ens et unum coincidunt* (or: *convertuntur*): (Entity and unity are the same [or: are interchangeable): anything properly characterizable as a thing must be a unit—that is, be specifiable (or identifiable) as a single item.

This is not merely a principle of ontology and should not be so understood in the present context. For here it does not concern the question: What is a thing like? Rather, it is a principle of communicative coherence: Whatever is to be meaningfully discussed needs to be identified—that is, specified in such a way as to distinguish it from the rest. Without specifying something as the particular item it is, you cannot put it on the agenda of consideration. The ruling precept is: "You cannot communicate successfully about something that you have not yet identified."

The principle in view is closely bound up with another: *nihil sunt nullae proprietates* (everything has some properties), seeing that identity stands coordinate with identifiability and requires descriptive specifiability, which in turn requires the possession of properties. (Observe, however, that the principle $E!x \rightarrow (\exists\phi)\phi x$ does *not* entail or require the converse: $(\exists\phi)\phi x \rightarrow E!x$. Pace the Bertrand Russell of "On Denoting," there is no good reason to deny properties to nonexistents—to deny that Pegasus, the winged horse, is winged.)[7]

Probative Principles of Rational Cogency

The principles at issue under this rubric are concerned to assure convincing argumentation. They are designed to provide for cogency in regard to philosophical evidentiation, demonstration, substantiation. Some classical instances are as follows:

#4

NOTHING IS WITHOUT A REASON. *Nihil sine ratione* (G. W. Leibniz). This has become known as the principle of sufficient reason.

With regard to principles in general, the medieval Schoolmen distinguished between an epistemological principle of knowing (*principium cognoscendi*) and an ontological principle of being (*principium essendi*). In this regard the present principle exhibits a typical duality. For it permits two very distinct constructions. It can be read in the light of Hegel's doctrine that the real is rational—that every aspect of the world's arrangements has its reason why. This, of course, is, as it stands, a very debatable bit of metaphysics.

But it can also be construed as a methodological precept from the practice of philosophy: MAINTAIN NOTHING SUBSTANTIVE WITHOUT GOOD REASON. Here its general effect would be that of the conjunction: "Be in a position to give a cogent reason for every doctrinal contention that you maintain. Refrain from making philosophical claims that lack the basis of a cogent rationale. Be in a position to support your contentions." This *methodological* (rather than *ontological*) construction of the precept clearly has the benefit of having much good sense on its side. After all, the object of a philosophical discourse is: to enlist the assent of (reasonable) interlocutors to a certain line of thought, which can only be done through substantiating a position.

#5

NOTHING COMES FROM NOTHING *Ex nihilo nihil* or *de nihilo nihil*. This was an ontological principle espoused by all the early Greek nature philosophers, according to Aristotle (*Physics* 1.4). Lucretius stressed the importance of this idea for his master Epicurus, who (according to Diogenes Laertius 10.24.38) based his physics on this self-same principle: *ouden ginetai ek tou mē ontos*. But this doctrinal principle of natural philosophy is also a methodological principle of philosophical reasoning. For, as readily happens in these matters, a principle of physical production comes to be transmuted into one of cognitive production. And so, just as substance must come from substance in the material world, so substantive conclusions cannot be rationally supported save by invoking substantive contentions in their support.

This principle is closely related in its general import to the legal precept *Qui exsequitur mandatum non debet excedere fines mandati* (He who executes a commission [charge, *mandatum*] must not go beyond its terms). In the context of philosophizing, this in effect says: When you draw implications and lessons from something already granted or established, do not exaggerate what this actually means. Do not go beyond the warrant of what has been established or conceded to you.

#6

(Even in reasoning) A CHAIN IS NO STRONGER THAN ITS WEAKEST LINK. *Non fortiter catena quam anulus debilissimus.* This too is true in the rational as in the physical realm. The idea was operative in the principle of Theophrastus in relation to modal syllogisms: the status of the conclusion is that of the weakest premiss: *Peiorem sequitur semper conclusio partem.* The conclusion always follows the weaker part (premise), not only the weaker in point of modality (as with Theophrastus),[8] but also the weaker in quality and quantity, with the negative understood to be "weaker in quality" than the affirmative and the particular "weaker in quantity" than the universal.

This weakest-link principle thus holds not only in the material world but in the realm of reasoning as well. A conclusion whose derivation requires a mixture of premises will itself be no more plausible than the weakest premise needed for its derivation. The obvious lesson is that in substantiating a philosophical contention we must strive to provide the strongest and best-established reasons we can manage to come by.

In a way, this principle is akin to *ex nihilo nihil*. For that principle requires that the premises be strong enough to yield the conclusion. And this principle stipulates that the conclusion must be weak enough to be sustained by the premises.

#7

(In forced choices) OPT FOR THE LEAST UNACCEPTABLE AL-TERNATIVE.. It is a familiar principle of moral philosophy that one should choose whatever course represents the least evil, as per the dictum of Cicero: *ex malis eligere minima* (*De officiis,* 3.1 3). But this idea obtains not just in ethics but in rational methodology as well. It finds an echo in the "Sherlock Holmes rule" that "When you have eliminated the impossible, whatever remains, however improbable, must be the truth."[9] And in philosophical contexts it has the application that one can substantiate a position by showing that all of its alternatives encounter problems and difficulties. For (and this is the critical principle) a position that, in comparison with its alternatives, encounters fewer and lesser difficulties than they do thereby deserves to be adopted—at least provisionally, until something better comes along.

Principles of Rational Economy

The principles at issue under this present rubric are concerned to assure efficiency in philosophizing. They are designed to avert needless labor both for the producer and for the consumer of philosophical work. Some paradigm instances follow.

#8

THE IMPOSSIBLE IS NEVER TO BE REQUIRED. *Ultra posse nemo obligatur.* No one is obliged to go outside the bounds of possibility: So taken, the principle is a variation on the legal dictum of Celsus the Younger: *impossibilium nulla obligatio est.* By its very nature, that which is impossible cannot be realized. In consequence, its realization cannot reasonably be demanded of anyone, the philosopher included. To show that it is impossible for a certain problem to be solved on the terms in which it is posed suffices to release the philosopher of any obligation to deal with it.

This principle is closely linked to another:

#9

IT IS ABSURD TO DEMAND THAT WHICH CANNOT BE HAD. *Est ridiculum quaerere quae habere non possumus* (Cicero, *Pro Archia,* 4.8). To insist on the realization of something acknowledged as in principle unrealizable is clearly irrational.

This principle has numerous philosophical applications. Skcepticism affords one example. If, as Descartes insisted, the human senses cannot, as a matter of principle, ever yield certainty about how matters stand in the world, then it would be absurd to insist on a concept of sensory knowledge that requires all-out certainty.

Again, if we agree with those moralists who maintain that moral perfection is something that it is in principle impossible for humans to achieve, then it will become absurd to insist on a conception of "a good man" that requires perfection for its applicability.

#10

NEVER EXPLAIN WHAT IS OBSCURE BY SOMETHING YET MORE SO. *Non explicari obcurus per obscurior.*

A satisfactory explanation must, of course, render matters clearer than they were to begin with. An explanation that violates the principle at hand will succeed at nothing other than obscuring the matter. The principle at issue implements the injunction: Never defeat your own purposes.

This principle has an obvious corollary:

#11

NEVER MAKE MATTERS MORE COMPLICATED THAN THEY HAVE TO BE. This is obviously a sound policy for procedure in philosophy as elsewhere. And this principle has the further, equally obvious corollary: NEVER EMPLOY EXTRAORDINARY MEANS TO ACHIEVE PURPOSES YOU CAN REALIZE BY ORDINARY ONES What is at issue here is a principle of rational economy: *non multiplicandae sunt complicationes praeter necessitatem.* This principle has the further corollary:

#12

ENTITIES ARE NOT TO BE MULTIPLIED BEYOND NECESSITY. *Entia non multiplicanda sunt praeter necessitatem.*

To all surface appearances, this looks to be an ontological principle, akin to, and perhaps even derivative from, "Nature does nothing in vain" (*Nihil frustra facit natura: hē phusis ouden poiei matēn*)[10] and even "Nature makes no leap" (*Natura non facit saltus*). However, such an ontological contention is *not* at issue here. For the principle in view should be construed methodologically. A brief look at its historical context is instructive in this regard.

The principle is widely attributed to William of Ockham. This attribution is highly problematic, however. For what Ockham himself actually had in view was a structure regarding not entities as such, but rather the methodology of rational procedure along the lines of

- *Pluralitas non est ponenda sine necessitate.*[11] Do not posit a plurality where a single item suffices.
- *Frustra fit per plura quod fieri potest per paucioria.* It is inappropriate to do with more what can be done just as well with fewer.[12]

Again, this is a principle of rational economy in relation to probative processes that is at issue.

#13

NECESSITY KNOWS NO LAW. *Necessitas non habet legem.* This maxim of natural law applies in philosophy as well. In proverbial wisdom it has such cognates as "Desperate times need desperate measures" or even "Any port in a storm."

Disaster in the present context is preeminently the catastrophe of contradiction. The history of philosophy is accordingly shot through with the use of distinctions to avert aporetic difficulties. Already in the dialogues of Plato we encounter distinctions at every turn. In book 1 of the *Republic*, for example, Socrates' interlocutor quickly falls into the following self-advantage paradox:

1. Rational people always pursue their own best interest.
2. Nothing that is in a person's best interest can be disadvantageous to his or her happiness.
3. Even rational people will—and must—sometimes do things that prove disadvantageous to their happiness.

Here, inconsistency is averted by distinguishing between two senses of the "happiness" of a person—namely, the rational contentment of what agrees with one's true nature and what merely redounds to one's immediate satisfaction by way of pleasure. In sum, the difference is between *real* and merely *affective* happiness. With real happiness, (2) is true but (3) false, while with merely affective happiness, (2) is false, but (3) is true. However much we would like to see happiness as a unified conception, the necessity of the situation constrains us to effect a partition.

#14

DO NOT BELABOR THE OBVIOUS. The root idea of this principles is operative in law (*de minimis non curat lex*), as well as in ordinary life: "Quit while you're ahead." Once your point is made or once your argument is developed with sufficient cogency for all practical purposes, call it a day. All this sort of thing is, of course, also simply a matter of sound practice in regard to the conservation of (intellectual) energy. This, too, is a principle of sound philosophizing, and indeed of rational procedure in general.

Closely related to this sensible prescription is yet another.

#15

NEVER FLOG A DEAD HORSE. Do not argue against that which nobody maintains. Let sleeping dogs lie, or, as Chaucer more eloquently put it, "It is naught good a sleeping hound to wake" (*Troilus and Creseyde*, 1.764). It is their heed of this consideration that accounts for the fact that sensible philosophers seldom trouble to refute such doctrines as panpsychism or solipsism.

Issues of Validation

Is the preceding inventory of philosophical principles complete? Of course not: no doubt the reader can think of other possibilities. All that this survey can lay claim to is that it registers principles that are both important and typical. Completeness lies only on the side of taxonomy—in the consideration that the principles at issue will relate to the understandability of the exposition, to its probative cogency, and to the rational economy of process.

Can principles conflict with one another? Are there mutually incompatible principles? Can philosophical conflict occur at the level of principles?

The answer, in briefest form, is no! There cannot be conflicting principles any more than there can be conflicting truths. It lies in the nature of the thing that where conflict occurs, there cannot be acceptability on both sides.

But, of course, we must, here as elsewhere, distinguish *what is* from *what seems to be*. The truth as such is self-consistent and conflict free, but this is not so with what people *think* to be the truth. And the same holds for principles as well. The salient point, then, is that insofar as we propose to maintain various maxims as principles—insofar as we propose to maintain various contentions as truth—we must make sure the consistency is preserved.

And here lies an important consideration. For there are not just principles but also *metaprinciples* that govern how one should operate with principles. And perhaps the most crucial of these is the (meta)-principle: KEEP YOUR PRINCIPLES CONSISTENT. The "principle of noncontradiction," that is to say, holds just as decidedly at the level of principles as at the level of assertions. And it, too, is in the end a principle of rational economy that holds up the interests, facilitating the purposes that are definitive of the rational enterprise at issue.

Are the principles at issue absolute and perennial or are they "epoch specific" (to use Whitehead's expression)? Are they inherent in the philosophical enterprise as such, or do they merely reflect the presumptions and predilections of a place and time?

As regards the particular examples canvassed above, it seems safe to lay claim to absoluteness. The reason for this lies in the purposive nature of philosophy as the discipline it is. For the aim of the enterprise is to resolve in a convincing way our big questions regarding reality and our place within it. And there is no point in endeavoring to do this in a way that does not effectively carry rational conviction—not just for people with the predispositions of a particular place and time but to sensible people in general. And this is exactly what those principles do (or should) endeavor to facilitate: their requirements reflect conditions under which alone the aims of the philosophical enterprise can be realized in an efficient and effective way. It is this serviceability for the very goal structure of the enterprise that endows those philosophical principles with their unconditional cogency.

This said, however, it must be conceded that the absoluteness of a principle does necessarily carry over to its implementation. Take the idea that one must never explain what is obscure by something that is yet more so. What sorts of things are obscure and what sort are clear will depend upon the state of knowledge and information of one's interlocutors. The negativity of the obscure is unconditional, but the *content* of the obscure—of just what is so and in which respects—is something that will be circumstantial and "epoch specific." In this regard, as in others, it can transpire that absolute principles call for circumstantially differentiated implementation.

Philosophers are supposed to be reflective and exhibit care and concern for what they themselves are doing. Nevertheless, the fact is that they only seldom consider the nature and basis of the methodological principles that govern their practice. They debate—and notoriously disagree—about the substantive issues, and thereby about how such methodological principles are to be applied in particular cases. But to judge by their practice, at any rate, they seem to be substantially agreed about the principles of appropriate procedure. (To be sure, some philosophers choose to refrain from argumentation altogether, but those that do present reasons and arguments for a position—that of position avoidance included—all pretty much adhere to the standard principles.) Why should this be? This question at once leads to another. How is the correctness or acceptability of philosophical principles to be established? How is one to evaluate a philosophical principle?

The first thing to note is that a philosophical principle is not a statement of fact but a rule of procedure. As such, its proper evaluation lies not in the range of what is itself a sound rule of practice:

> Any rule of practice or procedure is to be evaluated not in the range of true-false but in the range of effective-ineffective with respect to its efficacy in relation to the purposes of the practice at issue.

Now, the proper way to assess the merits of anything that is procedural or methodological in nature is in terms of its efficacy in realizing the objectives at issue—that is, in terms of its capacity to achieve the purposes of the procedural context at issue. The underlying idea is that of coming to the realization that to isolate the rule is to risk (and perhaps even assume) failure to achieve the objectives of the enterprise. A *functional* approach to evaluation is thus in order here.

As this perspective indicates, the validation of a procedural principle turns on the issue of purposive efficacy. And in this light, the process of validating a methodological principle turns on a line of reasoning of the following format:

> If you violate the principle in question, then you impede the realization of one of the characteristic aims of the enterprise at issue.

This circumstance explains why principles—like the Ten Commandments—can always be cast or recast as negative injunctions: "Thou shalt not . . ." In some of the preceding cases this may not be obvious at first glance. For example, "A chain is not stronger than its weakest link" does not look like a negative injunction. But, of course, it is. For it effectively comes to the proscription: Do not ask a chain to support more than its weakest link can bear."

Accordingly, it emerges that the validation of a philosophical principle will proceed along the following lines: If the principle is violated, then

1. It becomes, if not impossible, then at least more difficult than it should be to obtain any answer at all to our philosophical questions.
2. The answer we obtain will plunge us into actual self-contradiction; or else
3. The answer we obtain, even though averting self-contradiction, is incoherent and fails to provide for cogent understanding of the issues.

On this basis, the factor that is evaluatively pivotal for philosophical principles is that of the aim and mission of philosophizing. And here we have it—at least in a first approximation—that the aim of philosophy is to provide cogent and convincing answers to "the big questions" that we humans have regarding ourselves and our place in the world's scheme of things.

The following injunctions are accordingly bound to figure prominently in regard to the characteristic aims of philosophy:

1. *Provide answers to those domain-definitive questions*—that is, propound and communicate information that conveys these answers. (We want answers.)
2. *Seek for cogency*—that is, fit those answers out with a rationale that attains cogency and conviction by way of evidentiation, substantiation, and demonstration. (We want not just answers but answers worthy of acceptance.)
3. *Strive for rational economy*, pursuing the tasks at issue in points 1 and 2 in a way that is rationally satisfactory—that is, in an efficient, effective, economical manner.

It is with respect to these three prime goals of philosophizing that there came into operation the principles at issue in the preceding threefold categorization—communicative adequacy, probative cogency, and rational economy.

And so, in sum, the best support for a philosophical principle comes into view when we look to the sanctions that attach to its violation.

Specifically, to validate of a philosophical principle it suffices to argue that violations will plunge us into ignorance, inconsistency, irrelevancy, incoherence, extravagance (in either sense of that term), and comparable undesirabilities. And it is exactly on this basis that the validation of the previously enumerated principles has proceeded.

Dealing with Objections

To be sure, someone might be tempted to complain as follows in reacting to the preceding suggestion of a functionally pragmatic approach to the matter:

> There is little or nothing in the justifactory factors you have just canvassed that is characteristic of the philosophical enterprise. After all, communicative adequacy, probative cogency, and rational economy of process are desiderata for virtually any rational enterprise.

The response is simply that this "complaint" is entirely correct—the situation is just as it states. The only fly in its ointment is that this is no occasion for complaint or objection. For the validation of those methodological principles of philosophizing lies exactly and precisely in the consideration that they involve the application to the characteristic mission of philosophizing of fundamental principles of rational procedure that are applicable across the whole range of our intellectual endeavors.

To be sure, this also delimits the utility of these principles. As noted, philosophical principles resemble the Ten Commandments in that they, too, provide essentially negative injunctions. What they do is to specify impediments to cogency. Their message is something to the effect: if you wish your efforts to substantiate a philosophical thesis or position to achieve rational cogency, then you must avoid doing certain sorts of things (inadequate grounding, needless complication, and the like). Due heed to appropriate principles will, accordingly, not assure good philosophizing and will do no more than help in averting poor philosophizing. To do the work well it is certainly necessary, but by no means sufficient, to avoid the specifiable sources of error. Philosophical principles do not produce an issue-resolving algorithm for this domain. Heed of those relevant principles will not solve those philosophical problems: it will do no more than prevent one's efforts at problem resolution from going awry.

It must also be acknowledged that in philosophy as elsewhere, principles, like general rules of any sort, do not incorporate the conditions of their own application. The implementation of such principles does not hinge not on its self-evidence, or on yet further (presumptively higher-level) principles, but is a matter of good judgment that takes the detailed features of particular cases of application into account. The establishment of appropriate principles is something that may itself involve other principles of higher order and can therefore be a matter of practical reason. But the application or implementation of a principle in a particular case will always be a matter that to some extent involves not just cogent rationality but good judgment. Exactly through being general, principles cannot avoid entry into the gray region of borderline cases and controversial applications (which does not, of course, alter the reality of a much larger area of clearly conforming and clearly violating cases).

In concluding, one salient point remains to be emphasized: Even in so theoretical and reflective an enterprise as philosophy it transpires that functional and thus essentially pragmatic considerations have a critical role to play. For philosophy, like any other rational endeavor, has its definitive aims and goals, and these can unquestionably be pursued in ways that are more effective and in ways that are less so.

So much, then, for principles that serve the aims of philosophy. But what of the procedures and methods that provide the instrumentalities for their implementation?

Chapter 2

Aporetic Method in Philosophy

Consistency and Apories

The methods of cogent philosophizing are rooted in the very aims of the enterprise. Philosophizing may "begin in wonder," as Aristotle said, but it soon runs into puzzlement and perplexity. We have many and far-reaching questions about our place in the world's scheme of things and endeavor to give answers to them. But generally the answers that people incline to give to some questions are incompatible with those they incline to give to others. (We sympathize with the skeptics, but condemn the person who doubts in the face of obvious evidence that those drowning children need rescue.) We try to resolve problems in the most straightforward way. But the solutions that fit well in one place often fail to square with those that fit smoothly in another. Cognitive dissonance rears its ugly head and inconsistency arises. And the impetus to remove such puzzlement and perplexity is a prime mover of philosophical innovation.

An apory is a group of contentions that are individually plausible but collectively inconsistent.[1] The things we incline to maintain issue in contradiction. One can encounter apories in many areas—ordinary life, mathematics, and science included—but they are particularly prominent in philosophy. For the wide-ranging and speculative nature of the field—the fact that it addresses questions we want to raise but almost dare not ask—means that the range of our involvements and commitments is more extensive, diversified, and complex here than elsewhere. For it lies in the nature of the field that

17

in philosophy we must often reason from mere *plausibilities,* from tempting theses that have some substantial claim on our acceptance but are very far from certain. And so it can transpire here that the theses we endorse are inconsistent—conflicting plausibilities rather than assured compatible truths. Thus, aporetic situations arise, circumstances in which the various theses we are minded to accept prove to be collectively incompatible.

Consider a historical example drawn from the Greek theory of virtue:

1. If virtuous action does not produce happiness (pleasure), then it is motivationally impotent and generally pointless.
2. Virtue in action is eminently pointful and should provide a powerfully motivating incentive.
3. Virtuous action does not always—and perhaps does not even generally—produce happiness (pleasure).

It is clearly impossible on grounds of mere logic alone to maintain this family of contentions. At least one member of the group must be abandoned. And so we face the choice among

1. Abandonment: Maintain that virtue has substantial worth quite on its own account even if it does not produce happiness or pleasure (Stoicism, Epictetus, Marcus Aurelius).
2. Abandonment: Dismiss virtue as ultimately unfounded and unrationalizable, viewing morality as merely a matter of the customs of the country (Sextus Empiricus) or the will of the rulers (Plato's Thrasymachus).
3. Abandonment: Insist that virtuous action does indeed always yield happiness or pleasure—at any rate, to the right-minded. Virtuous action is inherently pleasure-producing for fully rational agents, so that virtue and happiness are inseparably interconnected (Plato, the Epicureans).

This illustration exemplifies the situation of an aporetic cluster: an inconsistent group of plausible contentions to which the only sensible reaction is the abandonment of one or another of them. Our cognitive sympathies have become overextended, and we must make some curtailment in the fabric of our commitments. Note, moreover, that in aporetic situations, unlike elsewhere, the option of a suspension of judgment is foreclosed; the mere rejection of a thesis is tantamount to the acceptance of its negation. For suppose that A, B, C is an inconsistent triad composed of theses we deem individually plausible. Then, by the hypothesis that we are minded "to accept as much as possible," when we drop C we are in a position to accept A and B, and these (by the condition of inconsistency) entail not-C.

Doing nothing is not a rationally viable option when we are confronted with a situation of aporetic inconsistency. Something has to give. Some one (at least) of those incompatible contentions at issue must be abandoned. Apories constitute situations of *forced choice*: an inconsistent family of theses confronts us with an unavoidable choice among alternative positions.

When one confronts an aporetic situation there are only two rationally viable alternatives: one can throw up one's hands, become a skeptic, and walk away from the entire issue, or else one can settle down to the work of problem solving, trying to salvage what one can by way of cognitive damage control and thereby make the best of a difficult situation. This latter course clearly has greater intellectual appeal.

Some Sample Apories

Apories—collective inconsistency among individually plausible contentions—structure the philosophical landscape. They show how various positions are interlocked in a mutual interrelationship that does not meet the eye at first view because the areas at issue may be quite disparate.

Consider, for example, the following apory:

1. All knowledge is grounded in observation (empiricism).
2. We can only observe matters of empirical fact.
3. From empirical facts we cannot infer values (the fact-value divide).
4. Knowledge about values is possible (value cognitivism).

Given that (2) and (3) entail that value statements cannot be inferred from observations, we arrive via (1) at the denial of (4). Inconsistency is upon us. There are four ways out of this trap:

1-Rejection: There is also nonobservational—namely, intuitive or instinctive—knowledge, specifically of matters of value. (Value intuitionism; moral-sense theories)

2-Rejection: Observation is not only sensory but also affective (sympathetic, empathetic). It thus can yield not only factual information but also value information as well. (Value-sensibility theories)

3- Rejection: While we cannot *deduce* values from empirical facts, we can certainly *infer* them from the facts by various sorts of plausible reasoning, such as "inference to the best explanation." (Values-as-fact theories)

4- Rejection: Knowledge about values is impossible. (Positivism, value skepticism)

Such an analysis brings out a significant interrelationship that obtains in the theory of value between the issue of *observation,* as per (2)-rejection, and the issue of *confirmation,* as per (3)-rejection. It makes strange bedfellows.

Again, consider the apory:

1. A (cognitively) meaningful statement must be verifiable in principle.
2. Claims regarding what obtains in all times and places are not verifiable in principle.
3. Laws of nature characterize processes that obtain in all times and places.
4. Statements that formulate laws of nature are cognitively meaningful.

As ever, various exists from inconsistency are available here, specifically the following four:

1- Rejection: Maintain a purely semantic theory of meaning that decouples meaningfulness from epistemic considerations.

2- Rejection: Accept a latitudinarian theory of verification that countenances remote inductions as modes of verification.

3- Rejection: Adopt a view of laws that sees them as local regularities.

4- Rejection: Maintain a radical skepticism with respect to claims regarding laws of nature, a skepticism that sees all such law claims as meaningless.

This apory locks four very different issues into mutual relevancy: (i) the theory-of-meaning doctrine that revolves about (1); the metaphysical view regarding laws of nature at issue in (2); a philosophy-of-science doctrine regarding the nature of natural laws as operative in (3); and finally a language-oriented position regarding the meaningfulness of law claims.

On Appraising Apories

When an apory confronts us with a forced choice among the propositions involved, it becomes unavoidable. One way or another we must "take a position"—some particular thesis must be abandoned or, at the very least, amended.

An apory thus delineates a definite range of interrelated positions. It maps out a small sector of the possibility space of philosophical deliberation. And this typifies the situation in philosophical problem-solving, where, almost invariably, several distinct and discordant resolutions to a given issue or problem are available, none of which our cognitive data can exclude in an altogether decisive way.

Consider a philosophical argument that supports a certain conclusion or contention C, on the basis of certain premises $P_1, P_2, \ldots, P_n$. (We may suppose, without loss of generality, that this argument is deductively valid, since if it were not we could treat it as enthymematic and supply the missing premises, so as to fill in the deductive gaps.) Note that if not-C does not have some modicum of plausibility, then it is scarcely worthwhile to argue for C. In philosophical argumentation one generally argues from contentions whose denials exert some appeal in virtue of having plausibility. (Even philosophers are disinclined to waste their time completely.) And so the series $P_1, P_2, \ldots, P_n$, not-C will form an aporetic family. The initial argument now reappears in a very different light. Instead of proving a conclusion from "given" premises, what we have is simply a collection of variously plausible theses that are collectively inconsistent.[2] We can thus subject the situation to the standard process of aporetic analysis.

Apories are not only frequent in philosophy but typical of the contexts in which the problems of the field arise. Accordingly, philosophical arguments can standardly be transmuted into aporetic clusters and analyzed in this light. In all such cases, a necessity for choice is forced by the logic of the situation, but no one particular outcome is rationally constrained by any considerations of abstract rationality. There are forced *choices* but no forced *resolutions*. Whenever we are confronted with an aporetic cluster, a plurality of resolutions is always available. The contradiction that arises from overcommitment may be resolved by abandoning any of several contentions, so that alternative ways of averting inconsistency can always be found.

This circumstance is typical of aporetic situations. Any resolution of an apory calls for the rejection of some contentions for the sake of maintaining others. Strict logic alone dictates only *that* something must be abandoned; it does not indicate what. No particular resolutions are imposed by abstract rationality alone—via the mere "logic of the situation." (In philosophical argumentation one person's *modus ponens* is another's *modus tollens.*) It is always a matter of trade-offs, of negotiation, of giving up a bit of this in order to retain a bit of that.

Thus, consider the following aporetic cluster:

1. Some facts can be explained satisfactorily.
2. No explanation of a fact is (fully) satisfactory if it uses unexplained facts.
3. Any satisfactory explanation must be noncircular: it must always involve some *further* facts (facts distinct from the fact that is being explained) to provide materials for its explanatory work.

Premise (3) indicates the need for unexplained explainers. Premise (2) asserts that the presence of unexplained explainers prevents explanations from being satisfactory. Together they entail that there are no (fully) satisfactory explanations. But premise (1) insists that satisfactory explanations exist. And so we face a contradiction. A forced choice among a fixed spectrum of alternatives confronts us. And there are just three exits from this inconsistency:

1. Abandonment: Explanatory skepticism. To refrain from accepting any explanation.
2. Abandonment: Explanatory foundationalism. To insist that some facts are "obvious" or "self-evident" in a way that exempts them from any need for being explained themselves and make them available as "cost-free" inputs for the explanation of other facts.
3. Abandonment: Explanatory coherentism. To accept circular explanations as adequate in some cases ("very large circles").

We have the prospect of alternative resolutions—but over a well-defined range of alternatives.

As such examples show, any particular resolution of an aporetic cluster is bound to be simply *one way among others*. The single most crucial fact about an aporetic cluster is that there will always be a variety of distinct ways of averting the inconsistency into which it plunges us. We are not just forced to choose, but specifically constrained to operate within a narrowly circumscribed range of choice.

But how to proceed? What is our standard of priority to be? Here we face a situation very different from that of reductio ad absurdum or of evidential reasoning. For in philosophy, our guidance for making these curtailments lies in the factor of systematicity. The operative principle at work here is that of achieving the optimum alignment with experience—the best overall balance of informativeness (answering questions and resolving problems) with plausibility by way of negotiating with the claims that on the basis of our relevant experience there is good reason to regard as true. We want answers to our questions, but we want these answers to make up a coherent systematic whole. It is neither just answers we want (regardless of their substantiation) nor just safe claims (regardless of their lack of informativeness) but a reasonable mix of the two—a judicious balance that systematizes our commitments in a functionally effective way.[3] The situation in philosophy is accordingly neither one of pure speculation, where informativeness alone governs conflict resolution, nor one of scientific/inductive inquiry where evidential coherence governs this process, but a judicious combination of the two.[4]

Of course, we could, in theory, in such a case simply throw up our hands and abandon the entire cluster. But this total suspension of judgment is too great a price to pay. By taking this course of wholesale abandonment we would plunge into vacuity by forgoing answers to too many questions. We would curtail our information not only beyond necessity but beyond comfort as well, seeing that we have some degree of commitment to all members of the cluster and do not want to abandon more of them than we have to. Our best option—or only sensible option—is to try to localize the difficulty in order "to save what we can."

Enter Distinctions

When an aporetic thesis is rejected, the usual course among philosophers is not to abandon it altogether, but rather to introduce a distinction by whose aid it may be retained *in part*.

Consider the following aporetic cluster, which sets the stage for the traditional "problem of evil":

1. The world was created by God.
2. The world contains evil.

3. A creator is responsible for all defects of his creation.
4. God is not responsible for the evils of this world.

On this basis we have it that God, who by (1) is responsible for all aspects of nature, by (3) is also responsible for evil. And this contradicts contention (4). Suppose, however, that one introduces the distinction between *causal* responsibility and *moral* responsibility, holding that the causal responsibility of an agent does not necessarily entail a moral responsibility for the consequences of his acts. Then for *causal* responsibility, (3) is true but (4) false. And for *moral* responsibility, the reverse holds: (4) is true but (3) false. Once the distinction at issue is introduced, then no matter which way one turns in construing "responsibility," the inconsistency operative in the apory at issue is averted.

Thus, someone who adopts this distinction can retain *all* the aporetic theses—(1) and (2) unproblematically and, as it were, half of each of (3) and (4)—each in the sense of one side of the distinction at issue. The distinction enables us to make peace in the aporetic family at issue, by splitting certain aporetic theses into acceptable and unacceptable parts.

Accordingly, one generally does not respond to cogent counterarguments in philosophy by *abandoning* one's position but rather by making it more sophisticated—by *complicating* it. One can never entrap any philosophical doctrine in a finally and decisively destructive inconsistency, because a sufficiently clever exponent can always escape from difficulty by means of suitable distinctions.

Apory Resolution as Cost-Benefit Analysis

Apories engender forced choices—choices that distinctions can mitigate but can never wholly avert. For what we need to do in order to effect a reasoned choice among the alternatives is to establish some *priority* or *precedence* among the data: to implement the idea that while they are all "acceptable" in a credibility-oriented sense, some are *more* acceptable than others. In situations of potential conflict, we must recognize that some have lesser claims on us for retention than others. Interesting ramifications lurk here.

In philosophy, the evidentially factual, purely cognitive constraints almost invariably underdetermine the resolution of our problems. To be sure, the cognitive-evidential situation is such that considerations of abstract rationality require us to make choices ("forced choices"). But there are no *forced resolutions*, for we are never constrained to a *particular* mode of inconsistency elimination in the cognitive situation at hand, at least not by considerations of abstract rationality alone. Concrete resolutions are always *underdetermined* by considerations of *cognitive* rationality; they become determined only when considerations of *evaluative* rationality come upon the scene. Philosophical problem-solving is, in the final analysis, an evaluative matter—though, to be sure, it is not aesthetic or ethical values that are at issue but specifically cognitive values that relate to matters of importance, centrality, significance, and the like. In philosophy, our problem resolutions always involve us in issues of precedence and priority. Cost-benefit parameters like "plausible" and "natural" come into prominence via such cognitive values as simplicity, economy, uniformity, harmoniousness, and the like.

The issue that we confront in apory resolution is thus one of priority—and ultimately one of *evaluation*. What it takes to resolve an apory is a matter of setting priorities—of substantiating a preferential choice, albeit one made on the basis of evaluative factors that relate to specifically informative matters. Probative values serve as the decisive factors here.

Are the evaluative judgments at issue ultimately *aesthetic*? By no means—at any rate as long as "aesthetic" means *affective*—let alone as involving matters of personal taste. Issues of procedural and cognitive value (simplicity, economy uniformity, etc.) are objectively descriptive features with regard to the organization and management of information—the systematization of experience, broadly conceived. Again, are those evaluative judgments not perhaps *ethical* in nature? By no means! To be sure, it would be *foolish* and counterproductive to fly in the face of those cognitive values—but not ethically improper or morally *wrong*. The salient point is that the domain of value is large and diversified, including beside the aesthetic and ethical also the cognitive, which relates specifically to those desirabilities that govern the rational use of information. And it is *these* values that are paramount in philosophical deliberation.

The resolution of apories is an exercise in cost-benefit analysis. No matter which way we turn in removing inconsistency, we pay certain costs in terms of thesis abandonment and concept complexification to achieve the benefits of retaining various aspects of the *status quo ante*. We pay the cost of complexification for the benefit of continuing our commitment to what seems "only plausible and natural" from a less reflective standpoint. Some appeal of a fundamentally evaluative nature is always ultimately involved. (This, ultimately, is why philosophical disputes are so recalcitrant.) But it is—or should be—values of a cognitively orientational bearing that are to be invoked.

Some readers may see such a position as having ominously skeptical implications for the status of philosophy—as undermining the validity of the whole enterprise. But this view will itself be based on a very questionable evaluative position. For the present deliberations regarding evidential underdetermination only indicate the indecisiveness of philosophical deliberations for someone who thinks that only resolutions founded on strictly evidential considerations are really worth having—that problem resolutions involving the invocation of cognitive values are somehow inferior, questionable, and not really worthwhile. Curiously enough, such disparagement of the evaluative domain itself represents a thoroughly evaluative posture—and a highly problematic one at that.[9]

The preceding deliberations serve to highlight the pivotal role of distinctions in philosophy. This business of distinction deserves closer examination.

Chapter 3

On Distinctions in Philosophy

What Distinctions Are

Distinctions are concepts used to effect a division among items in line with real or perceived significant descriptive differences among them. Thus, truly meaningful distinction should not merely reflect a difference but a *real* or *genuine* difference: in the language of Plato's *Phaedrus* and *Sophist*, a distinction (*dihairesis*) should "cut nature at its joints." Ideally, a distinction would reflect a significant contrast in the operational or functional nature of the items at issue. In the scholastic terminology still used by Suarez, it should be real (*distinctio realis*) rather than merely mental (*distinctio rationis*), representing a difference in the things themselves rather than merely in how we think and talk about them. (Think here of the distinction between paintings and sculptures, on the one hand, and between good paintings and bad paintings, on the other.)

Fundamentally there are two sorts of distinctions: *identifying* distinctions and *classifying* distinctions. Identifying distinctions are those that dichotomously distinguish the Xs from the non-Xs. Classifying distinctions are those that sortally distinguish the Xs from the Ys (and possibly from the Zs and Ws as well). Classifying distinctions presuppose identifying distinctions. For if we cannot even identify the Xs by distinguishing them from the non-Xs, we obviously cannot confidently hope to be successful in distinguishing the Xs from the Ys.

From a logical point of view, distinctions are closely bound up with generalizations. For one thing, to succeed in distinguishing the Xs from the Ys we must have it that "All Xs are non-Ys" (and conversely).

27

Moreover, there is no point to and no prospect of a generalization of the form "All *X*s are *Y*s" if we cannot distinguish the *X*s from the non-*X*s or the *Y*s from the non-*Y*s. The Aristotelian categories, for example, that differentiate the sorts of question one can raise about things (What? When? Where? Why? etc.), will only make sense if we have the means for distinguishing one relevant base (e.g., when questions) from the rest.

In view of their dichotomous nature, identifying distinctions are synoptic, thanks to their aspiration to exhaustiveness: whatever it be, an item is either an *X* or a non-*X*. However, classificatory distinctions are generally drawn with respect to a limited range of objects. Even so basic a distinction as animal/vegetable/mineral is drawn only with respect to *physical* objects: numbers, say, or colors do not fall within its scope. Only rarely is a classificatory distinction synoptic—that is, drawn with respect to things or items in general, irrespective of kind. In general, classification proceeds by kinds and succeeds sortalization.

Moreover, a meaningful distinction will always be drawn with regard to some respect (even as sameness—the opposite of difference—is differentiated in point of respect, as per "the same age" or "the same shape"). Thus, we can draw distinctions between, say, animals in point of construction (backbone or nonbackbone), in point of habitat (wild or domesticated), in point of diet (meat-eating or noncarnivorous), or in point of use (beast of burden).

The identifying distinction between *X*s and the non-*X*s can accomplish its intended work in being smoothly and unproblematically applicable only when the world is duly cooperative. The essentially ontological requirement that is at issue here means that the *X*s constitute a natural kind in that nature affords a descriptively determinate manifold of items—a natural category, as it were—to which the *X*s belong. A proper distinction must have a rationale—a rational basis that constitutes an appropriate ground for the distinction—that is traditionally characterized as the *fundamentum divisionis*.

In noting that *cognition* is *re-cognition*, psychologists have long stressed the fundamental role of distinctions in human cognition. In the nineteenth century Alexander Bain proclaimed in his "law of relativity"—(actually, "law of contrast" would have been better) that all awareness—all human consciousness and thought—consists in the noting of differences, with the concepts at issue in distinctions providing the requisite instrumentalities.[1] However, it is specifically the role of distinction in philosophy that will be the focus of concern in the present discussion.

In this context, one particularly important distinction was initiated by the philosophers of ancient Greece who divided the range of fact into two components: those that obtain by nature (*physis*) and those that obtain by convention (*nomos*). This classical distinction between facts in general bears specifically upon distinctions as well. Their being drawn by people is a matter of artifice, of convention with respect to some purpose or other. But their efficacy for the purpose at hand is an objective, nature-determined fact that exerts the objective impetus of quality control over our conventional proceedings.

How Distinctions Fail

The process of distinction confronts the reality that whenever the phenomena reflect a continuous series of shadings, any point of division is bound to be arbitrary, failing to provide for the clear separateness needed for effective distinctions. Furniture ages one day at a time, so when does it begin to be "antique"? A person ages and develops one year at a time, so when does someone suitably develop to qualify as being "of age" in point of maturity for marriage or for voting? An aggregation of grains of sand grows one grain at a time, so when does it qualify as constituting "a heap"? Just this phenomenon of continuity engenders difficulty for distinctions, thanks to what might be called applicative variability. After all, one individual is mature at age twelve while another fails to be so at twenty-four. One individual is an old man at fifty while another is quite spry and youthful at seventy. In such cases there is no natural line of separation, no clearly appropriate way of effecting distinctions. Whenever issues of sheer contingency arise, nature just does not afford convenient joints for our distinctions to cut.

All the same, a society must often make artificially separating determinations in the interests of an efficient and effective conduct of its business. For reasons of administrative convenience it must resolve by the artifice of lawful fiat that which nature does not decide in a natural and principled way. Voting age, drinking age, age of consent for contracts or for marriage, and the like all effect an essentially procrustean determination that determines by conventional fiat that which nature leaves undetermined. So here distinctions are defective, because they do not strictly abide by the rules.

Distinctions can fail either through *formal flaws of definition* or through *material flaws of application*.

Formal flaws of definition arise when the very meaning of what is involved in being an *X* is indecisively determined and the concept itself fails to be well-defined. The principal flaws of this sort are imprecision, nonexclusivity, and nonexhaustiveness. They arise as follows:

Formal Flaws of Distinction

- *Imprecision*: An attempt to distinguish Xs from other items is bound to fail when the Xs are not delineated with precision. For example, a distinction between fated and non-fated occurrences or between usual and unusual occurrences will be virtually useless until such time (if ever) when the conditions of being fated or of being usual are appropriately specified.
- *Nonexclusivity*. The classificatory distinction between Xs and Ys is nonexclusive when there are items that are—or seem to be—both Xs and Ys. Thus, the distinction between sea creatures and mammals is vitiated by the existence of whales which are both. The very fact of nonexclusiveness shows that the distinction is flawed in failing to "cut nature at the joints."
- *Nonexhaustiveness*. Classificatory distinctions can also fail through lack of exhaustiveness. For example, the distinction between random and lawfully necessitated occurrences is nonexhaustive, because occurrences that are governed by probabilistic laws are neither lawfully necessitated nor random. The distinction between works of fact and works of fiction is vitiated by works that purport to be factual but have substantial fictional components or vice versa.

The material flaws of distinction in point of applicability are mainly three: vacuity, triviality, and pointlessness. They arise as follows:

Material Flaws of Distinction

- *Vacuity*. The distinction between Xs and non-Xs—or between Xs and Ys—fails in point of applicability when there just are no clearly identifiable Xs so that the group is vacuous. An example would be the distinction between spectral and substantial beings or between witches and nonwitches.
- *Triviality*. A distinction between Xs and Ys is trivial if there just are no significant differences between the two. When this happens and whatever differences there are are insignif-

icant, then the distinction is also said to be "merely virtual," "quibbling," and, more picturesquely, "pettifogging."

- *Pointlessness.* A distinction between the *X*s and *Y*s is pointless when, even though there is some notable difference between the two, this difference serves no further explanatory or instructive function (as, for example, the contrast between days whose dates are prime numbers and those that are not). Such a distinction has no larger implications in point of cognitive utility. There is a significant difference in color between red things and green things (between tomatoes and sunsets, on the one hand, and lawns and unripe apples on the other). But no further purpose is served by drawing this distinction, which lumps together objects that have no further significant features in common.

Ockham's razor had it that "entities are not to be multiplied beyond necessity: *entia non praeter necessitatem multiplicanda sunt.*" And just this also obtains for distinctions. Distinguishing is only a meaningful measure where a significant context-relevant advantage results. The lack of functional utility typified by pointlessness is among the principal ways in which distinctions can fail.

While distinctions can commit error of commission through being flawed and inappropriate, there is, however, also the other side of the coin—to wit, the errors of omission arising through a failure to draw appropriate distinctions in not distinguishing between things that are significantly distinct. This sort of error of putting together things that should be kept apart is generally characterized as confusion or conflation.

So much for the nature of distinctions and their problems. Let us now turn to the crux of our present concerns: their role in philosophy.

Misassimilation

A fallacy of misassimilation results from the running together of things that should be kept apart. This, of course, is one of the gravest errors that can be made in regard to distinctions.

To misassimilate is to ignore a necessary distinction by unifying into a single item (kind, entity, process, idea, or whatever) things that are different in kind and distinct in character; to treat such significantly distinct things uniformly amounts to riding roughshod over significant differences. Misassimilation is an invitation to error. For it underwrote the mistaken idea that a uniform account—a monolithic analysis or explanation—is possible where quite different situations actually prevail. We become enmeshed in a confusion—a mistaking of what is a mere analogy or a mere similarity as a ground for claiming an identity of nature. A fallacy is thus at issue, because one is now led to saying of one thing what only holds for another.

To render the idea graphic, it helps to think of what is going on here as a kind of cognitive myopia. Thus someone who is unable to distinguish (say, on an eye chart) between E and H might as a result of this visual deficiency impose a spurious order on the reading series

   E H E E H H H H E H . . .

by seeing this as

   E H E H E H E H E H . . .

Or conversely he might impose on an orderly series of this sort the randomness reflected in that initial series. Cognitive myopia, just like visual myopia, engenders either conflict or confusion.

At the conceptual level at issue in philosophical deliberations misassimilation can result whenever there is in fact an insignificant circularity between concepts or ideas to sustain their appropriate unification. Specifically, this will result under the following conditions:

- There is only an imperfect analogy that is sufficient to sustain actual identification.
- There is only a family resemblance among the items at issue rather than a pervasive unity of aspect.
- The coordination between the items at issue is the product of mere connection rather than an uniformity of nature.

Uniformity of treatment is appropriate only where there is a uniformity of nature—a functional sameness based on an uniformity (isomorphism) of comportment or constitution that leaves no room for item-destabilizing distinctions.

Uniformity in such cases is simply an optical illusion. Misassimilation links together items that are fundamentally desperate. The flaw is one of oversimplification through ignoring the subtleties of differentiation. Misassimilation leads to the deeply mistaken idea that in the case at hand a one-size-fits-all account is practicable.

Regrettably, this sort of thing occurs all too often in philosophy.

One example of a plausible candidate for the title of misassimila-tion is the idea of causality. Many philosophers talk as though "X causes Y" would be accommodated through a uniform explanatory account, perhaps along the lines of "X happened in the wake of Y, and without Y's happening, X would not have happened." But a zillion scenarios can be constituted that would falsify this. (Example: "The dropping of water from the trees during the rainstorm cause the patio to get wet.") The idea of causality is just too many-sided for any one account to hold good. There is, after all,

- the causality of physical process ("The sunshine caused the water to evaporate")
- the causality of psychological reaction ("The insult caused his cheeks to flush")
- the causality of intention ("The dog's growling caused the cat to stop in her tracks")
- the causality of problematic connection ("His drinking caused the chances of an accident to increase")

There are just too many different ways in which one process or level or state can be bound up with various results for any account of causation to be viable across the board. That one word "cause" is simply too versa-tile for one account of its modus operandi to be viable.

The idea of evidentiation and evidence affords another example of potential philosophical misassimilation. For the idea at issue exfoliates in a plethora of different directions. We have

- the evidence of our senses (sight, touch, etc.)
- the evidence of a witness (eyewitness testimony)
- evidence secured via deductive or inductive reasoning from given data
- documentary evidence

To be sure, there is something in common here in that all of these varied forms of evidence serve to provide grounds for believing (or dis-believing) something to be the case. But the discussion to believe—like the decision to marry—is something that can be based upon so wide a variety of different grounds and reasoning that there is nothing in common apart from the result produced.

The idea of knowledge affords another example of philosophical misassimilation. To begin with, there is the obvious distinction between performative how-to knowledge (how to open a can with a can opener; how to hit a backhand in tennis) and factual knowledge (that Paris is the capital of France; that the Empire State Building has more than sixty stairs). But even with just the latter there are problems. Various theorists to the contrary notwithstanding, there just is no one uniform account to explain "*X* knows that *p*," which, after all, would be used for any one of the following sorts of things:

- *X* would say yes if asked, "Is *p* the case?"
- *X* has at times accurately thought *p* to be the case
- *X* has entertained thoughts from which p can be derived (or: can be derived easily)

To be sure, it is understandable why misassimilation should occur in such cases, seeing that what is at issue instantiates the grammatical phenomenon of polysemy that occurs when a single word does a considerable variety of (generally interrelated) jobs.

One common way in which misassimilation comes into play is that which might be termed the misintegration that expresses itself by speaking of "the *X*" where what is actually at issue is a complex and diversified plurality. Thus, it makes no sense to speak of "the ground of World War I" or "the cause of the common cold" or "the invention of the automobile" or "the reason for eating a good diet." In such cases there just is no one factor that plays the role allocated to it by that unifying "the." And so in philosophy to ask for "the rationale of morality" or "the meaning of life" is to get the discussion off to a wrong start by prejudging the issue via a problematic presumption of morality. And similarly we encounter in contemporary philosophy a widespread proliferation of "the" locutions. "The skeptic maintains *X*," "The empiricist holds *Y*," and so on. There is a plethora of skeptical and empirical positions, and only some of them maintain *X* or hold *Y*. The flaw of insufficient specificity manifested in such locutions is yet another way in which misassimilation becomes operative.

To assimilate—to cosortalize under one common rubric—is to vouch for the idea of significant commonalities, of a cover sameness or identity of condition. And when there is misassimilation this implicit promise is simply not fulfilled, because critical distinctions have been overlooked or neglected. The proper cure for this sort of thing is, of course, only too obvious. One must take care to draw the appropriate distinctions.

So much for the nature of distinctions and their problems. Let us now turn to the crux of our present concerns: their role in philosophy.

Historical Background

Medieval thinkers stressed the difference between *real* or *substantive* distinctions and the merely conceptual distinctions imposed by ways of thinking and talking—the so-called rational distinctions. The difference became increasingly prominent, particularly in the wake of the writings of St. Thomas Aquinas. On its basis, the distinction between the long days of summer and the short days of winter is real—incorporated in the solar system's modus operandi. But the distinction between holy days and ordinary days is purely conceptual—inherent not in the phenomena themselves but only in the ways people think and act about them.

To be sure, the *domain* of a distinction, its intended range of intended applicability, comes to play a key role here. Thus, in distinguishing *colors* it is crucial to distinguish green from nongreen. But in distinguishing *objects* there is little point in insisting on distinguishing the green from the nongreen: classing green objects together—frogs, lawn, unripe apples, and so forth—would be a pointless exercise.

In developing this line of thought, Duns Scotus divided meaningful distinctions into three groups:[2]

1. *Distinctiones reales,* real distinctions: distinctions between concrete things or, concrete substances. The Eiffel Tower can accordingly be differentiated from the Tower of London.
2. *Distinctiones rationis,* distinctions of thought or conception: distinctions between different ways of conceiving things. For the selfsame thing may be thought of under different descriptions, even as Socrates may be conceptualized as "the master of Plato" or "the husband of Xanthippe."
3. *Distinctiones formales,* or formal distinctions: distinctions between objects in terms of their nature or essence. Thus, cats and dogs differ by nature (*ex natura rei*).

The later medieval philosophers elaborated this sort of classificatory scheme greatly and reveled in drawing ever more complex distinctions between different sorts. And various parts of the Scholastic theory of distinctions was taken over into Renaissance neo-scholasticism and figures significantly in such twentieth-century philosophers as Descartes and Spinoza.[3] In particular, Leibniz with his principle of the identity of indiscernibles taught that items are different when they cannot be intersubstituted—that is, they cannot be interchanged in our claims without sometimes affecting their truth status (*salva veritate*). But this idea that items are different when different things can be said about them needs to be qualified and sophisticated. For when mere thought-distinctions are at issue in modal claims regarding the same object, this claim is falsified. Take Frege's example: Venus the Morning Star is also the Evening Star. But while "The Morning Star is necessarily the Morning Star" is clearly true, "The Morning Star is necessarily the Evening Star" is not. And when "John liked thinking about the Morning Star" is true, "John liked things about the Evening Star" may not be. There is no distinction of reals here, but the impact of modality effects a distinction of reason.

This line of thought leads to our principal theme: the role of distinctions in philosophy.

The Role of Distinctions in Philosophy

Distinction is a prime instrument of damage control in philosophy. Philosophy endeavors to answer "the big questions" regarding the place of man in the world's scheme of things. And in doing so it begins by framing its questions in the ordinary concepts of everyday communication. And when the questions that arise are posed in the terms of reference afforded by everyday concepts, then it is only reasonable and proper to provide answers within the same conceptual framework, seeing that those answers (if answers they are) must address *those* questions. But here the difficulty begins. For the world's complexity is such that we are never able to achieve a perfect fit here, because the world's phenomena are so complex and variegated that there will always be problem cases that just do not fit smoothly into the concepts and patterns that characterize the general run of things. And so, in their striving for maximum generality the generalizations of philosophy are virtually always overgeneralizations involving a certain amount of oversimplification. For if "All Xs are Ys" is an overgeneralization, then it must transpire that some Xs—certain extraordinary ones—will not be Ys. And in taking these into account an inconsistency is bound to result.

Accordingly, distinctions are particularly prominent in philosophy, because in the interests of generality the theorists of this domain are given to overgeneralization. But whenever they propose a generalization of the format "All *X*s are *Y*s," an opponent all too readily springs to the fore with an example of *X*s that just are not *Y*s. And at this point distinction becomes a natural axiomatic measure. Our theorist goes on to say:

> I spoke somewhat hastily. It is not, of course, the case that "all *X*s are *Y*s"; rather it is the *X*s of type 1—the ordinary *X*s—that are *Y*s. The type-2 *X*s—the contextually extraordinary ones—can indeed fail to be *Y*s.

And so a thematic shift from

> All *X*s are *Y*s

to

> All *X*s are *Y*s

effectively salvages (much of) that initial generalization through recourse to the distinction between the type-1 *X*s and those of type 2.

Restoring consistency among the incompatible beliefs calls for abandoning some of them as they stand. However, philosophers resist consistency restoration by resorting to the brute force of outright rejection. When a philosophically plausible contention runs into problems through the emergence of counterexamples, philosophers do not abandon their theories. Rather, they have recourse to *modification*, replacing the problematic thesis with a duly qualified revision thereof. They salvage their theses by introducing distinctions.

The history of philosophy is shot through with distinctions introduced to avert the aporetic difficulties inherent in oversimplification. Already in the dialogues of Plato, the first systematic writings in philosophy, we encounter distinctions at every turn. In book 1 of Plato's *Republic*, for example, Socrates' interlocutor quickly falls into the following apory:

1. Rational people always pursue their own interests.
2. Nothing that is in a person's interest can be disadvantageous to him.
3. Even rational people sometimes do things that prove disadvantageous.

However, the evident inconsistency that arises here can be averted by distinguishing between two senses of the "interests" of a person—namely, the real and the apparent, what is *actually* advantageous to him and what he merely *thinks* to be so. Again, in the discussion of "nonbeing" in Plato's *Sophist*, the Eleatic stranger traps Socrates in an inconsistency from which he endeavors to extricate himself by distinguishing between "nonbeing" in the sense of not existing *at all* and in the sense of not existing *in a certain mode*—that is, between absolute and sorted nonexistence. Throughout, the Platonic dialogues present a dramatic unfolding of one distinction after another.

Again, there is a potential conflict between the sociopolitical distinctions of welfare utilitarianism and individual rights. The former calls for measures serving the greatest good of the greatest number ("the public good") and the latter for respecting the fundamental rights of individuals. But what happens when the best interests of many call for riding roughshod over the just claims and rights of a few? Clearly, the viability of theory now calls for introducing suitable distinctions. For instance, we can now no longer measure the good of individuals in terms of a materialistic "standard of living" but have to look also to the *quality* of life in a larger sense, which includes living in a society that respects individual rights and secures the legitimate claims of individuals.

Distinctions enable the philosopher to remove problems of inconsistency not just by the brute negativism of thesis *rejection* but by the more subtle and constructive device of thesis *qualification*. The crux of a distinction is not mere negation or denial, but the revision of an untenable thesis into something positive that does the job better.

For example, consider the following aporetic cluster of individually tempting but collectively inconsistent theses:

1. All events are caused.
2. If an action issues from free choice, then it is causally unconstrained.
3. Free will exists—people can and do make and act upon free choices.

Clearly, one way to avoid inconsistency is simply to abandon thesis (2). We might well, however, do this not by way of outright abandonment but rather by speaking of the "causally unconstrained" only in Spinoza's manner of *externally* originating causality. For consider the result of deploying a distinction that divides the second premise into two parts:

2.1   Actions based on free choice are unconstrained by *external* causes.

2.2   Actions based on free choice are unconstrained by *internal* causes.

Once (2) is so divided, the initial inconsistent triad (1)–(3) gives way to the quartet (1), (2.1), (2.2), (3). But we can resolve *this* aporetic cluster by rejecting (2.2) while yet retaining (2.1)—thus in effect *replacing* (2) by a weakened version. Such recourse to a distinction—here that between internal and external causes—makes it possible to avert the aporetic inconsistency and does so in a way that minimally disrupts the plausibility situation.

And this is typical in philosophy. For whenever aporetic inconsistency breaks out, one can thus salvage our philosophical commitments by *complicating* them, by making revisions in the light of appropriate distinctions, abandoning them altogether.

❦

Distinctions enable us to implement the idea that a satisfactory resolution of aporetic clusters must somehow make room for all parties to the contradiction. The introduction of distinctions thus represents a Hegelian ascent that rises above the level of antagonistic positions to that of a "higher" conception in which the opposites are reconciled. In introducing the qualifying distinction, we abandon the initial thesis and move toward its counterthesis, but we do so only by way of a duly hedged synthesis. In this regard, distinction is a "dialectical" process.

This role of distinctions is also connected with the principle that is sometimes designated as "Ramsey's maxim." With regard to disputes about fundamental questions that do not seem capable of a decisive settlement, Frank P. Ramsey wrote: "In such cases it is a heuristic maxim that the truth lies not in one of the two disputed views but in some third possibility which has not yet been thought of, which we can only discover by rejecting something assumed as obvious by both disputants."[4] On this view, too, distinctions provide for a higher synthesis of opposing views. They prevent thesis abandonment from being an entirely negative process, affording us a way of salvaging something, of "giving credit where credit is due" even to those contentions we ultimately reject. They make it possible to remove inconsistency not just by the brute force of thesis rejection, but by the more subtle and constructive device of thesis qualification.

A distinction reflects a *concession*, an acknowledgment of some element of acceptability in the thesis that is being rejected. However, distinctions always involve us in bringing a new concept onto the stage of consideration and thus put a new topic on the agenda. They accordingly always afford invitations to carry the discussion further, opening up new issues that were heretofore conceptually inaccessible. Distinctions are the doors through which philosophy passes into new topics and problems. New concepts and new theses standardly come to the fore in the wake of further distinctions.

Philosophical distinctions are thus creative innovations. There is nothing routine or automatic about them—their discernment is an act of inventive ingenuity. They do not elaborate preexisting ideas but introduce new ones. They not only provide a basis for understanding better something heretofore grasped imperfectly, but they shift the discussion to a new level of sophistication and complexity. Thus, to some extent they "change the subject." (In this regard they are like the conceptual innovations of science, which revise rather than explain prior ideas.)

The continual introduction of new concepts via new distinctions means that the ground of philosophy is always shifting beneath our feet. New distinctions for our concepts and new contexts for our theses alter the very substance of the old theses. The development is dialectical—an exchange of objection and response that constantly moves the discussion onto new ground. The resolution of antinomies through new distinctions is a matter a of creative innovation whose outcomes cannot be foreseen.

While distinctions serve to avert conflict, nevertheless they always leave a crucial evaluative issue hanging in the air: the issue of *priority*. The pivotal question always arises, given that the term T can be split apart into the two senses T_1 and T_2, which of these two captures the "standard" or "normal" use of the word? Which construction is it that we should generally give to the equivocal word when we meet it in the relevant discussions? (For example: is it belief-as-true or belief-as-plausible that is at issue in standard cases?) Which sense *predominates*?

Consider the following apory:

1. Only observationally verifiable sentences are (genuinely) meaningful. (Positivism.)
2. The speculative claims of traditional metaphysics are not observationally verifiable.
3. The speculative claims of traditional metaphysics are meaningful. (Metaphysical traditionalism.)

Given that (2) is "fact of life," we are driven to a choice between (1) and (3). Now a peacemaker might propose a distinction here, offering the following proposal:

> Let us introduce the (somewhat technical) idea of *empirical* meaningfulness—that is, let us distinguish between what is empirically meaningful ("experientially resolvable" in some way) and what is not. Then one can accept (1) and abandon (3) in this particular sense, while retaining (3) and abandoning (1) with respect to "loose, old-fashioned meaningfulness-at-large."

But it is clear that such a distinction, which enables us to "have it both ways," will not really make peace between the metaphysical traditionalist and his positivist adversary. Even while agreeing to "split the difference" in the face of the distinction, the positivist will say in his heart: "It is *empirical* meaningfulness that really counts, it is in this that true-blue authentic meaningfulness consists." The metaphysician, however, will say: "This idea of '*empirical* meaningfulness' is a mere technical construction that is really beside the point. It is meaningfulness-at-large that captures the authentic core of the idea." There is now a fight, of sorts, for the right to the succession. Each of the new distinction-generated conceptions seeks to establish itself as the principal heir of the root concept. The quarrel now becomes one of which side represents the prime, main, most important aspect of the root distinction-antecedent idea? The issue becomes of evaluation—of emphasis and priorities.

Philosophical Apories Tie Issues Together

In philosophical epistemology the need arises to come to grips with the following *paradox of explanation*:

1. *Principle of sufficient reason*: Every fact needs and (in principle) has a satisfactory explanation.
2. *Principle of noncircularity*: No fact is self-explanatory. And none can appropriately figure in its own explanatory regress.
3. *Principle of comprehensiveness*: No explanation of a fact is satisfactory so long as (any of) its explanatory materials themselves go unexplained.
4. But then, since the facts at issue at any stage of the explanation must be explained, and this explanation itself requires

something new and yet unexplained (by (4), it follows that no fact can ever be explained satisfactorily.

5. Statement (4) contradicts (1).

Here (1)–(3) constitute an inconsistent triad. At least one of the plausible principles of this aporetic cluster has to be abandoned in its unqualified generality. There are three exits from this situation:

> 1-rejection. This involves the acceptance of surds, of brute facts that must be accepted without themselves having or needing explanation.
>
> 2-rejection. This allowing some facts to play a role in their own explanation—perhaps by adopting a nonlinear ("coherentist") model of explanation that distinguishes between vicious and virtuous explanatory circles.
>
> 3-rejection. This involves accepting an explanation as satisfactory once it reaches a point where the materials at issue are substantially clearer and more perspicuous then the fact being explained—a point where sufficient explaining has been done that we are entitled to call it a day.

Three very different philosophical positions are involved here: surdism, coherentism, and explanatory pragmatism. And it is clear that the apory at issue interlocks them into a coordinated interrelationship.

Consider the *freedom/causality paradox* of the following aporetic cluster, which sets the stage for controversy about freedom of the will:

1. All human acts are causally determined.
2. Humans can and do act freely on occasion.
3. A genuinely free act cannot be causally determined—for if it were so determined, then the act is not free by virtue of this very fact.

These theses represent an inconsistent triad in which consistency can be restored by any of three distinct approaches:

> 1-rejection: This is "voluntarism"—the exemption of free acts of the will from causal determination (Descartes).
>
> 2-rejection: This is "determinism" of the will by causal constraints (Spinoza).

3- rejection: This is "compatibilism" of free action and causal determination—for example, via a theory that distinguishes between inner and outer causal determination and sees the former sort of determination as compatible with freedom (Leibniz).

Again we have a variety of philosophical positions interlocked through their common role in an aporetic situation. And in this case the issues can be addressed by disentangling our knotted terminology through suitable distinctions.

Their grounding in aporetic conflicts provides philosophical controversies with a natural structure that endows their problem areas with an organic unity. The various alternative ways of resolving such a cognitive dilemma present a restricted manifold of interrelated positions—a comparatively modest inventory of possibilities mapping out a family of (comparatively few) alternatives that span the entire spectrum of possibilities for averting inconsistency.[5] And the history of philosophy is generally sufficiently fertile and diversified that all the alternatives—all possible permutations and combinations for problem resolution—are in fact tried out somewhere along the line.

Philosophical doctrines are accordingly not discrete and separate units that stand in splendid isolation. They are articulated and developed in reciprocal interaction. But their natural mode of interaction is *not* by way of mutual supportiveness. (How could it be, given the mutual exclusiveness of conflicting doctrines?) Rather, competition and controversy prevail. The search of the ancient Stoics and Epicureans (notably Hippias) for a universally "natural" belief system based on what is common to different groups (espousing different doctrines, customs, moralities, religions) is of no avail, because no single element remains unaffected as one moves across the range of variation. Given that rival "schools" resolve an aporetic cluster in different and discordant ways, the area of agreement between them, though always there, is generally too narrow to prevent conflict. An alternative position has different priorities, and different priorities are by nature incompatible and irreconcilable.

Chapter 4

Respect Neglect and Misassimilation as Fallacies of Philosophical Distinctions

Respect Neglect

Our concern here is with the error that may be characterized as the fallacy of respect neglect, an error that is particularly common among philosophers. It is a prominent instance of the broader fallacy of illicit amalgamation, which consists in treating as a single uniform unit something that in fact involves a diversified plurality of separate issues. Specifically, it has the form of treating a feature F as a unified property that things do or do not have, whereas in fact F has several respects, and things can have F in one respect and lack it in another. There are many instances of this phenomenon—for example, the *simplicity* of scientific theories, the *preferability* of objects of choice, and the *fairness* of decision processes.

Clearly, some characterizing features of things are monolithic and categorical, a matter of yes/no and on/off. And act is either legal or not; a task, either feasible or not. But, equally clearly, this is not always the situation that prevails.

Some features are maxirespectival: To have F you must have it in *all* respects: if something fails to be F in a single respect, then it is not F at all. Perfection is like that, as is the justice of an action or its legality or its honesty or its courtesy.

Other features are miniperspectival: To have F it suffices to have it in *some* respects: if something has F in even a single respect, then it flatly has *F*. Imperfection and injustice are like that, as is the generosity of an act or its impropriety.

It is easy to see that in denying features that are maxiperspectival or in ascribing features that are miniperspectival, we can afford to neglect respects. But, of course, not all features will be like that.

Moreover, it may also happen that there is respectival dominance where one single factor is by itself all-determinative. Survivability-geared safety from destruction is an example: If we do not survive in the short run, there is no use worrying about matters further down the road. But it is not easy to think of other examples of this sort where one single respect-dimension is so predominant and able to speak for the totality that a proliferation of respects does not come into it. But many important features of things are neither mini- or maxiperspectival. Here the proliferation of respects becomes critical, and the fallacy of respect-neglect arises when this critical consideration is ignored.

Let us consider some examples, beginning with the concept of simplicity.

Simplicity

Simplicity has certainly played a prominent role in twentieth-century philosophy of science—especially in methodologically governed discussions of reductive reasoning. From C. S. Peirce to Rudolf Carnap and Hans Reichenbach and beyond, philosophers of science have seen the simplicity of theories as a key factor for their acceptability.

All the same, it is clear on even casual inspection that the idea of simplicity in relation to theories splits apart into a proliferation of respects. There is.

- *expressive simplicity*: syntactical economy in the conceptual machinery of formulation
- *instrumental simplicity*: simplicity in terms of the amount of mathematical apparatus needed for formulating the theory (mere algebra, calculus, complex function theory, etc.)
- computational simplicity: how easy it is to compute results and outcomes by use of the theory
- *pedagogical simplicity*: how easy it is to teach the theory and to learn it

And the salient point is that we here encounter a diversified manifold of perspectives from which one theory can be seen as simpler than another.

It is an important consideration that these different modes of simplicity are not necessarily in agreement. Consider an analogy: the simplicity of automobiles. One can be simpler than another in point of

- being easier to manufacture
- being easier to maintain
- being easier to start
- being easier to drive

And these can and actually do conflict with one another. A car that is easier/simpler to manufacture is not necessarily one that is easier/simpler to drive. Moreover, even these factors themselves proliferate further. The "easier to drive" will split apart into "in dry conditions," "in wet conditions," "on smooth and well maintained roads," and so on. With automobiles, simplicity is critically respectival. And the simplicity of theories is in much the same situation.

To say that one object—be it a theory, an auto, an action, an idea, a belief, or whatever—is simpler than another is perfectly proper and meaningful, but only if one specifies some particular respect or aspect. Here one cannot appropriately speak of simplicity *tout court*. And to fail to acknowledge that simplicity is subject to fission into a plurality of respects that may potentially even conflict with one another is to succumb to what might be characterized as the fallacy of respect neglect.

Fallacy

It would be futile to seek to escape the fallacy of respect neglect by seeking to have it that *real* simplicity is a matter of being simpler in *every* respect, so that respectivization becomes irrelevant. But this is all too often decidedly impracticable. But, of course, whenever different respects are mutually conflicting—as we see in the automobile example—there will be no workable way of taking this step. And this situation is only too common.

Political theorists of democratic inclination often maintain that in matters of social decision the preferability of alternatives is to be decided by the choices of individuals. Philosophers of science maintain that in matters of theory choice, the preferability of alternatives is to be decided by the explanatory merit of theories. But the eligibility of items from the standpoint of individuals may well be (and all too often is) a matter of respect, with A being preferred to B in one regard and B to A in another—and neither respect predominating over the other. And the explanatory merit of theories in one regard (e.g., generality) and range of applicability may be at odds with their explanatory merit in another (such as ease of application).

Merit and preferability in all applications of their idea are matters of respect. Take something as simple as a house. Clearly, one may be superior to another in location, roominess, circulation, solidity, and so forth. And this sort of situation obtains with matters of social policy as well.

Take equality—another theme that is currently popular with political theorists. Equality can be a matter of opportunity, of treatment, in the distribution of goods and bads, and so on. And here too there can be conflicts. In giving each holder of a lottery ticket an equal chance at the prize, we preclude sharing it equally by different holders.

Again, take the idea—popular with some philosophers of science—that scientific theories are equivalent when they have the same mathematical structure. This could perhaps be made to work if the idea of structure were a respect-free monolith rather than respectival. But just as a sentence expressed in language has a grammatical structure, a lexicographic structure, a theoretic structure, a rhythmic structure, and so forth, so a scientific theory has many sorts of structure. And indeed, even a given mathematical fact can find its expression in ways that differ substantially in structure. (The structure of the expression of the fact that two plus two is four is very different in the arithmetic of *Principia Mathematica* and in its formulation by Gödelian means.)

Hermeneutic theorists occasionally embark on the quest for correct interpretation. But clearly the real question is not "Is there a single right interpretation?" as per a recent book of that title.[1] For to ask if there is one single right interpretation (of a literary or philosophical text, a painting, etc.) is to invite the fallacy of respect neglect. To pose a genuinely meaningful question one would have to ask, "Is there one single interpretation that is optimal in a certain particular specified respect." And here the correct answer is that rather uninteresting response: sometimes yes and sometimes no. After all, that original question is muddled through the fact that interpretations have different aspects, different respects. Interpretation can be geared to the intentions of the author, to the general understanding and expectations of the audience, to the issue of utility for our own problems, and so on. And it is effectively impossible—in principle as in practice—that one single interpretation can be right or optimal in every respect.

Such deliberations point to a general conclusion. Committing the fallacy to respect neglect invites unhappy consequences—confusion if not outright self-contradiction. And this is not only in the case of the particular issue that presently concerns us—simplicity—but involves a whole host of other cases as will (preferability, similarity, utility, predictability, importance, testability, etc.).

It might be thought that respective fusion or amalgamation is the cure for respect proliferation. It is not. Thus, suppose some good or bad is to be allocated among several equally deserving parties. Then there is fairness of opportunity, fairness of result, or fairness of process. In point of result, it seems unfair to allocate the entire item to X rather than Y. But if this was determined by a spin of the roulette wheel, then there was fairness of opportunity. On the other hand, if the good was divisible and could have been shared out in equal portions, then it would be unfair to allocate it by lot. But of course, the case of indivisible goods shows that one cannot reply that (categorical) fairness is simply a matter of being fair in every respect, seeing that here realizing fairness is one respect may preclude the prospect of realizing it in another.

Whenever a higher-level factor of desirability—such as that of simplicity or economy or convenience—fissions into a plurality of different respects or aspects these will often (perhaps even generally) prove to be combination resistant. Consider the analogy of ease and convenience in the context of food. This is clearly something that is subject to respect proliferation: food can be easier to produce, easier to prepare, easier to digest, or easier to acquire. A food that is easy to prepare for eating (e.g., a ripe banana) will not be easier to come by if we don't live in a banana-growing region. A food may well need more complicated preparation (e.g., cooking) if it is to be easier to digest. And so on. There is no way in which one food can be easier overall than another, because the various respects of ease will conflict with one another.

And just the same sort of situation is going to obtain in the case of such concepts as similarity or preferability or the like. All of them dissolve into a plurality of respects that will themselves have yet further respects. And—most relevantly for our present purposes—this is going to hold for simplicity as well. A respect-involving notion like those just mentioned is going to be inherently diversified, subject to different aspects that cannot simply be forced together in smooth coordination, because more of one of them will be obtainable only at the price of less of another.

And this internal diversity stands in the way of amalgamation even as the inner tension among the various rational aspects of simplicity precludes one thing's being simpler than another in every potentially relevant respect. There will be no way of fusing the different aspects into one unified overall result. For since the simplicity—in our present case—is inherently respect-localized, it fails to admit a global, symphonically unified version. There will be simplicity (or preferability, or similarity, etc.) in this or that respect, but no such thing as an all-around, unrestrictedly global realization of the idea. And to insist on overlooking those manifold discordant respects is to prelude the realization of anything meaningful. The complex realities of the case block the prospect of integrative fusion, of overall unification.

The problematic nature of respect neglect is rooted in the fact that we cannot in general make absolutes out of comparatives. One leaf may be greener than another, but there is no such thing as an absolutely or categorically green leaf. One rock may be harder than another, but there is no such thing as an absolutely hard rock. One route may be more easier than another, but there is no such thing as an absolutely or categorically easy route. Against this background the move from comparative to absolute simplicity—or equality, or preferability, and so on—becomes deeply problematic.

Nor can we generally make categoricals out of respectivals. A sentence may be awkward in this or that respect, but it cannot be unrestrictedly awkward. A tool may be useful in this or that respect, but it cannot be unqualifiedly useful. One task can be more challenging than another in this or that respect, but it cannot be unconditionally challenging. One thing can be simpler than another in this or that respect, but it not only will not but cannot be categorically (unrestrictedly, unqualifiedly, and unavoidably) simple.

The long and short of it is that respect neglect is a common pitfall in philosophical deliberations. No fault or flaw is more ominous in philosophy than falling into self-contradiction. And when something obtains in one respect and not in another, then (as Aristotle already insisted)[2] in neglecting the respect involved and riding roughshod over the differences involved, we all too readily fall into contradiction and thereby become unable to do that to which philosophers must always aspire: to talk sense.

Chapter 5

Systemic Interconnectedness and Explanatory Holism in Philosophy

The Problem

The difficulty of establishing neat boundaries of distinction and broad generalities of doctrine in philosophy originates in the intricacies and complexities inherent in the issues. These complications mean that the issues have to be addressed in their systemic interrelatedness. It would, of course, be agreeable and convenient if this complex whole could be broken up into neatly separable parts. But this is unfortunately not the case here. To see the reason why, it helps to begin with the question: Does explaining the existence of the parts explain the whole?

David Hume apparently thought so. In his *Dialogues Concerning Natural Religion*, Hume's foil, Demea, asks whether it is conceivable that the world as a whole can arise through a self-generative process in the manner of a biological species through the generation or reproduction of its plants or animals. Hume's Philo replies: "Very easily. Even as a tree sheds its seeds into neighboring fields and produces other trees, so the great vegetable, the world, or this planetary system, produces within itself seeds which, being scattered into the surrounding chaos, vegetate into new worlds."[1] Evidently, Hume thought that the existence of the universe as a whole would be explained seriatim via an explanation of the production of its constituent parts. He formulated his position as follows:

> Did I show you the particular causes of each individual in a collection of twenty particles of matter, I should think it very

unreasonable, should you afterwards ask me, what was the cause of the whole twenty. This is sufficiently explained in explaining the cause of the parts.[2]

And echoing Hume, Paul Edwards declares that "It is . . . absurd to ask for the cause of a series as a whole as distinct from asking for the causes of its individual members."[3] And so there has come to view a principle, sometimes characterized as the Hume-Edwards thesis, to the effect that "if the existence of every member of a whole is explained, the existence of that whole thereby also explained." This thesis has found sporadic endorsement, and various theorists deem it acceptable.

But G. W. Leibniz had thought otherwise.

Even if we should imagine the world to be eternal, still, the reason for it would clearly have to be sought elsewhere, since we would still be assuming nothing but a succession of states, in any one of which we can find no sufficient reason, nor can we advance the slightest toward establishing a reason [for the whole], no matter how many of these states we assume. . . . The reasons for the world therefore lie in something extra-mundane, different from the chain of states or series of things whose aggregate constitutes the world.[4]

Who is right on this issue? To get a good grip on this question, we are well advised to go back to fundamentals.

Summative Features

A feature is *mereologically summative* if it can be projected from applying to the parts of a whole taken distributively to applying to that whole collectively. Accordingly, mereological summativity centers on the formula: "Whenever all of the parts of a whole are F, then that whole is F as well."

The feature F is thus mereologically summative if it transpires that whenever all the parts comprising a certain whole X have the feature F, then X will do so as well. Instances of mereologically summative features are afforded by color and composition. For we clearly have it that "If all the parts of something are green, then so is that thing itself," and "If all the parts of something are made of iron, then so is that thing itself." By contrast, there will of course be mereologically nonsummative features such as size, shape, weight. For clearly we do not have "If all the parts are small, then the whole will be small."

In this context, the idea of a whole and its parts is of course diversified—wholes can be spatial, temporal, discursive (as with a book and its chapters), cognitive (as with an argument and its stages), and so on. Many properties are such that mereological summativity fails. The circumstance that every brick is well-made does not mean that the wall they comprise is well-made. The fact that every one of its words is short (familiar, readily understood) does not mean the book is short (familiar, readily understood). It is clear that the question of mereological summativity will very much depend on the particular feature that is at issue.

Fallacies of Composition and Division

A fallacy of composition consists in implementing the inferential step with mereological summativity that is at issue with a conditional of the format "If all the parts of X have F, then X itself will also have F" in cases where this is inappropriate and erroneous. This fallacy is thus committed whenever one mistakenly takes a feature that is not summative to be so. For example, we cannot indicate that a committee is wise from the fact that all of its members are, nor that a story is thematically well developed if all of its paragraphs are. Nor—to take J. S. Mill's example—do we have it that if each part of a set is affordable, the set as a whole willbe so.[5]

The inverse of the fallacy of composition is the fallacy of division, based on the formula "If a whole has a certain property F, then all of its parts do." Many properties will engender this fallacy. For instance, the fact that all its members are American does not mean that an organization is so as well—it could very possibly be incorporated in Canada. Nor can we say. "The regiment survived the battle to fight another day, therefore all of its members survived" or "The club has ceased to exist, therefore its members have ceased to exist."

Is Existence Mereologically Summative?
No—A Whole Is More Than Its Parts

It is clear that a whole need not share the features of its parts. Every human has a mother, but that does not mean that humankind at large does so. But what about existence? If the parts exist must not the whole do so as well? And does not the explanation of the existence of these parts thereby achieve an explanation of the existence of the whole?

Clearly, this does not obtain in general! For it very much depends on whether we are dealing with a mere aggregate or a genuine whole that has some sort of structure. We have an *unstructured* collection when there is simply a set of parts; a *structured* whole adds something to this— namely, an organization or specific mode of combination. Even as a watch or an automobile is more than the mere aggregate of its components, so any structured whole is more than the mere aggregate of its parts. And when a whole of some kind comes to be what it is through having the parts ordered in some particular structural interrelationship, then the mere existence of these parts is not enough to ensure existence of the whole.

The thesis that the whole simply is the totality of its component parts (or that "The world is the totality of existing things") is equivocal. It is true and unproblematic in the sense that the world has no parts or components over and above those that do in fact constitute it. But it is certainly false if construed to deny that the world has aspects or features of a structured sort that characterize it—features that if changed would change the whole even if the parts were just the same. The words *PIT*, *TIP*, and *IPT* have the same constituent letters but are far from being the same word.

The Analytical/Constructionist Program

In the larger setting of metaphysics as a whole, the particular methodological program of what might be characterized as constructivist metaphysics envisions an atomism that is predicated on two premises:

1. The complex objects of consideration can be disassembled analytically into constituents of greater simplicity.
2. The iteration of this process of disassemblage will ultimately terminate in objects of maximal simplicity, resulting in basic constituents that effectively serve as atoms.

This philosophical program had its origins in pre-Socratic times in the teachings of Leucippus and Democritus. And their *physical* atomism had its parallel in the *mathematical* atomism of Greek geometry that culminated in the Euclidean construction of geometric facts by means of proofs from atomistic axioms. The impressive success of this program in science and mathematics over the years has exerted a pervasive and enduring influence that one can see at work throughout the history of philosophy. And in the twentieth century it came into particular prominence. Four prime instances of this phenomenon may be cited.

Instances of the Implementation of the Constructionist Program

Exhibit A: Logical Atomism (Russell-Wittgenstein)

Logical atomism was contemplated by Ludwig Wittgenstein in his early *Notebooks* (1914–16). At the time it seemed clear to Wittgenstein that logic is committed to a theory of *simple objects*, because without logical simples to work with, the combinatory mechanisms of logic will find no grist for their mill. After considering different possibilities for what these objects could be—for example, minimal sensibilia or even points in visual space[6]—Wittgenstein settled on atomic propositions. Thus, he wrote:

> The simple for us is: the simplest thing we are acquainted with, the simplest thing to which analysis can attain. It need appear only as a prototype (*Urbild*), as a variable in our sentences. It is this [i.e., something we cannot analyze further] that we intend and seek.[7]

In the final analysis (no pun intended) logic cannot get by without such simples, seeing that "the meaning (*Bedeutung*) of our statements is not unendingly complicated."[8]

Nonetheless, there remains the difficulty of specifying just exactly what these ultimate simples are. While acknowledging the difficulty of resolving this problem, Wittgenstein thought it could be solved by an egg-of-Columbus maneuver whereby and could specify not necessarily where it *must* stop but where it *does* stop. The simple is simply what we *treat* as simple in our logical proceedings: simplicity emerges where we care to analyze matters further. Thus, Wittgenstein thought he could obtain what he needed without really settling the question of what these simples are as such.

In his later paper entitled "Logical Form"[9] Wittgenstein tried to do better. He envisioned the construction of an ideal language revealing the "logical form" of facts by showing how the statements regarding them result from the concatenation of atomic propositions. The basic problem of philosophy, as he then saw it, was to clarify the nature and substance of these atomic propositions. And the solution lies in looking for those bits of discourse that are devoid of any logical structure—those, that is, which we de facto treat as simple.

Wittgenstein's program was fostered by Bertrand Russell. Under Wittgenstein's influence he developed his "philosophy of logical atomism"[10] over the 1915–25 decade. For Russell, too, the guiding idea was that there are certain fundamental facts that are constitutive of all facts at large—the so-called logical atoms or atomic facts. Such atomic facts either attribute universals to individual observable items (presumably, sense data) (as per "this visual impression is red") or relate such items to each other (as per "this visual impression succeeded that one"). Atomic facts are thus the constituents of all facts at large, so that all propositions are either atomic (basic or simple) or else molecular (i.e., composite or complex) by way of construction from atoms. Russell's theory was closely akin to that being developed by Wittgenstein, and it is difficult to separate out exactly what each of them owed to the other.

Mention must also be made of the later idea of a dialectical atomism at issue in the program of mathematico-logical constructionism developed by Paul Lorenzen. This is based on the idea of developing a game-theoretic semantics based on basic dialectical steps of challenge and response to assertions in a sort of dialogical game. Here the basic atoms are bits of argumentation that constitute an exchange of challenge and response.[11] Such a program represents a logical atomism of argument-moves rather than of statements as such.

In any event, however, the program of philosophical atomism soon ran into difficulty. For the issue of how to clarify the nature of the atoms at issue soon emerged as the major problem for philosophical atomism. Those concerned claimed to know *that* there are logical simples without being able to specify to anyone's satisfaction what they are. In the end, the theorists of the program were never able to find a solution of this problem that satisfied even themselves—let alone others.[12]

And so metaphysical atomism came to look in other directions.

Exhibit B: Process Atomism

A. N. Whitehead's philosophy of process, as expounded in his 1929 masterwork, *Process and Reality*,[13] was one of the most important and influential metaphysical doctrines projected in the twentieth century. Now, be it rightly or wrongly, some process theorists regard it as a fundamental feature of Whitehead's thought that there are in nature elemental atomic processes from which all other processes can be constituted. They see Whiteheads's "actual occasions" as themselves altogether indecomposible units that serve as building blocks out of which all larger processes are then constituted in successive layers of concatenation. (Whether Whitehead himself held such a view is discussable but by no means certain.) Accordingly, in shifting from a metaphysics of substance to one of processes one almost still retains the ancient atomistic approach geared to ultimate units of existence. Abandoning substantialism in favor of processism—a radical step, indeed—they nevertheless retained the classical atomism of the older metaphysical school that traced its roots deep into Greek antiquity.

Now, such a process atomism is certainly the theoretical possibility. But it is also a problematic proposition—and one that is rather at odds with the spirit of a philosophy that sees process itself as fundamental. Why, after all, should process be seen as in discrete units? Why should the succession of processes constituted by subordinate processes inevitably have to come to an end? Clearly, atomistic processism involves a questionable concession to the thoroughly process-estranged point of view of a constructionism from ultimate units—process exempt from processes, as it were. Surely, it would ultimately be more plausible to contemplate a Chinese-box-like succession of larger processes embracing ever small ones, along the lines of the poet's idea of larger fleas having ever smaller ones to bite 'em—ad infinitum. After all, if nature is indeed processual, then why should not its composition be processual "all the way through"?

Among process atomists there is a tendency to think that genuine novelty requires atomicity—that originality must come in discrete jumps, in patentable units, so to speak. But this looks to be an aspect of the specifically human condition that need surely not be projected into the metaphysics of reality at large. Why should there be ultimate particles of process that are nowise resolvable into more basic constituents? From the process point of view, it is surely only natural to envision reality as a manifold of concatenated processes that admit—in principle—of decomposition into ever-smaller processual units; a pervasively structured manifold of micro- and macroprocess whose intricacy is unlimited and does not come to an end is a rock bottom of some sort that is itself exempt from the process of decomposition that we find at work everywhere else.

Then too, philosophical atomism has also taken some other directions in the twentieth century.

Exhibit C: Epistemic or Cognitive Atomism
(Carnap and the Vienna Circle)

The *logical* atomists of the Wittgenstein-Russell school were interested in the analysis of meaning: theirs was a semantical atomism that looked to have units of meaning. By contrast the *cognitive* atomists of the stripe of Carnap and the Vienna Circle were interested in the analysis of evidentiation: theirs was a probative atomism that looked to basic units of evidentiation or verification of factual claims.

The idea of cognitive atoms is, of course, old hat. Thus, as the Scottish school of "common sense" thinkers saw it, the question "How do you know that *p* is true?" sets afoot a regress of substantive reasons that must always ultimately terminate in "basic," elemental, nonevidentially self-evident propositions. The idea that this is a process that we carry on only as long as we *need* to—that is, only until we reach a point at which additional substantive reasons (while not unavailable) cease to be less problematic than the claims for which they are adduced—is a notion that did not figure in *their* thinking (but that of course is no reason why it should not figure in *ours*). In the first half of the twentieth century, such a cognitive atomism made a notable comeback—this time in relation to science rather than to common sense.

For Moritz Schlick knowledge is the product of units of experience from which in the end—in natural science, for example—certain structural features were abstracted. Cognition thus roots ultimately in the mental processing of elementary units of experience.

Rudolf Carnap sought to fit this line of thought out with systematic rigor.[14] To be sure, Carnap too was interested in "primitive" concepts (to be found, in the Russell-Wittgenstein manner, in "primitive ideas" as backed by "primitive relations"). But for Carnap the "primitive ideas" were not (as per Russell) terms that characterize the data of sense, but rather momentary cross-sections of the stream of experience. By a complex coordination (*Aufbau*), these atomic units of knowledge combine to constitute cognitive units from which the yet more complex compounds that represent our empirical knowledge can be amalgamated.

Otto Neuarth sharply criticized this sort of approach. He rejected the whole quest for "atomic" or primitive or "basic" units of knowledge as the remnant of the metaphysical search for "ultimate foundations." And even if a semantical program along these lines is accepted, there will be no viable transition to the epistemological plane. Knowledge is not a constitute for several atoms but a complex web for which verification emerges at the end rather than something that qualifies as a report from the very start. So even if we were to accept certain concepts as atomic, basic, or undefined primitives in a linguistic context so that our language is seen as a construction, this program does not carry over to our body of scientific knowledge.

The net effect of Neuarth's critique was to bring the epistemic atomism of Carnap and his Vienna followers to its end. For, as Neuarth sensibly insisted, there is no way of specifying these cognitive atoms in such a way that any plausible mode of constructive synthesis can be found that is able to yield scientific knowledge as we have it.

Exhibit D: Action-theoretic Atomism

Let us turn, finally, to action-theoretic atomism. This was a doctrine that had a wide following among philosophers in the 1960s.[15] Instructions tell us how to accomplish a complex action by presenting a recipe of sorts: first do this, then that, then that. But some actions look to be elemental: we can instruct someone to do them, but cannot tell them how to do so by disassembling the action into yet more elementary components. We cannot provide someone with a set of instructions for, say, "breathing in" or "sticking out one's tongue" or "blinking one's eyes." Such actions are generally characterized as "basic" or even "atomic" in that they appear to lack component parts. Nor need such conditional basic actions be bodily movements: "imagining a triangle" or "recalling a face" will also afford illustrations.

For one thing, it is hard to say what an ultimate unit of action could be. It is easier, however, to present putative examples of basic actions than to give an adequate exposition of what such actions are.

One starts the car by turning the key, but for the experienced driver there are not two separate actions of turning the key and of starting the car with the former sensory as a component of the latter. To move one's finger one must first move it halfway, but it is hard to see how this movement is a component of the former, since moving those muscles never enters one's mind at all.

The problem besetting action-theoreticationism is basically the same as that which brought to grief all the other forms of metaphysical atomism in the twentieth century: the inability to come up with clearly viable candidates for the key role of atoms.

₿

As these examples indicate, twentieth-century philosophy has seen a substantial extension of the classical physicalistic atomism across a wide section of the philosophical landscape. For the tradition of analytical philosophy took the analogy of chemical analysis seriously. Seeking to implement this approach, its devotees sought to analyze complex objects into their "simpler" constituents and ultimately to reach the end of the line in absolutely simple (i.e., nondecomposible) elemental atoms.

Problem Number One: The Fallacy of Termination Presumption

The fact of the matter, however, is that the atomistic metaphysic exemplified in all these various approaches faces encounters some problems. It faces the prospect of two serious—and potentially fatal—sorts of obstacles. A closer look at these is not only of historical interest in relation to the atomistic program but carries wider and still relevant lessons for the cogency of philosophical deliberation at large.

The first and prime problem of philosophical atomism is that with any given mode of decomposition, it may well prove infeasible to reach an end of the line. In disassembling a complex object of consideration there may very possibly be an atomic stopping point, but we may also face the prospect of an ongoing regress that potentially continues in infinitum. This envisions an analysis that is nonterminating and extends "all the way down," so to speak. In this event there will be a failure of atomism, thanks to an absence of atoms.

Take the case of process atomism, for example. In the final analysis there is no sound reason why the decomposition of processes into subordinate subprocesses must at some stage reach its end in nondecomposable atomic process and can not continue *ad indefinitum*. Moreover, even if processes are arranged at different levels of descriptive complexity, then it is possible that we will have atomicity at any given level, while nevertheless the shift to another level of consideration would allow reduction to further subordinate processes at a deeper level. Thus, conscious process might reach an end in atomistically indecomposable conscious acts that themselves, however, admit of subconscious disaggregation, or life-processes that admit of organically atomic processes that themselves nevertheless consist of subordinate preorganic (electrochemical) processes.

In principle, all the various modes of philosophical atomism—and in particular logical atomism, cognitive atomism, and action-theoretic atomism—are open to exactly the same sort of objection. There is no need to suppose the existence of ultimate units of meaning, of knowledge, or of action. It is perfectly plausible to suppose that in each case the analysis into more elementary constituents can always be carried further, and that when we stop the process—as we must—we do so because there is no *need* rather than no *possibility* of carrying matters any further. But this assumption is deeply problematic in its reliance on the potential error at issue here, which might be termed *the fallacy of terministic presumption*.

To be sure, within the narrow context of a limited inquiry addressed to a particular and specific issue the process of sequential analysis may well reach its end in the realistic circumstances of concrete cases; but this is seldom if ever, because we have come to the end of the theoretical line in an atomic bedrock of ultimate reality. Instead, the termination is contextual: It is (to reemphasize) not that there is no *possibility* of carrying the analysis further, and when we stop it may be from exhaustion and not by necessity.

Accordingly, the idea that a somehow simpler, more elementary component may well be implementable without underwriting the idea of simples that are absolute and ultimate may fail us. There just may not be an atomistic end of the line. In this way, simplicity and constituency are always comparative and never absolute. For where there is no end of the line, we will always have to speak of one thing's being simpler than another. Simplicity becomes an ineluctably comparative rather than a qualitatively descriptive concept.

Problem Number Two: The Disintegration of Simplicity and the Fallacy of Respect Neglect

The concept of an atomic level ultimately reached by analytical decomposition also runs into another significant obstacle. For the resolution of a complex into its purportedly simpler constituents foundered on the realization that there is such a thing as one constituent being flat-out simpler than another. The traditional route to atomistic metaphysics absolutizes the idea of comparative simplicity in a way that is deeply problematic. But something is never flatly more simple than another, but only simpler in this or that respect. Simplicity itself is a complex conception that disassembles into a proliferation of distinct constituents. The idea of overall, everything-considered simplicity—of being totally simple—becomes impracticable, because nothing is simpler in every way. And this clearly creates a big problem for the idea of re-sorting an object into its more elemental constituents.

How is one to implement the idea of one action being a "more elemental component" of another? After all, the very idea of componenthood is a problem. For the idea of one action's being a constituent component of another can be construed spatially, or temporally, or spatiotemporally, or structurally, or procedurally (thus, as regards structure, if "standing at attention" is to count as an action—as it must—then "keeping one's heels together" is part of it).[16]

To fail to acknowledge that simplicity is subject to a pluralizing fission of respects that may potentially even conflict with one another is to succumb to what I characterized in chapter 4 as the fallacy of respect neglect. And it would clearly be futile to seek to escape from difficulty here by claiming that *real* simplicity is a matter of being simpler in *every* respect, so that respectivization becomes irrelevant. For whenever different respects are mutually conflicting, there will be no practicable way of taking this step.

Any concept that is respect-relativizable poses the danger of committing the fallacy of respect neglect. So here, too, there looms a major obstacle to metaphysical atomism.

Perspectival Dissonance and Nonamalgamation

In the end, the need for respectivism in a multifaceted world means that the quest for irreducible simples comes to grief on the fact that we cannot in general make absolutes out of comparatives. One leaf may be greener than another, but there is no such thing as anything absolutely or categorically green. One rock may be harder than another, but there is no such thing as an absolutely hard rock. One route may be easier than another, but there is no such thing as an absolutely or categorically easy route. Against this background the move from comparative to absolute simplicity becomes problematic.

These deliberations carry a significant lesson. To have a variable atomism of ultimate simples in the face of the theoretical problems that have been under consideration here one must take two steps:

1. One must avoid respect neglect, since the idea of atomicity comes to grief when the analysis into ultimately simple constituents has to be *respectivized.*

2. One must avoid, *termination presumption* inherent in the idea that the process of analysis or decomposition must terminate in a dead end.

These two considerations combine to indicate the fatal flaws of twentieth-century metaphysical atomism.

To all visible appearances, atomicity can accordingly be contemplated only within this or that particular purposive setting. Atomicity is thus something that is determined not by what a thing *is* but by how it is *treated*—a feature that depends not just on it but also on us. It is—to reemphasize—*functional* rather than *ontological*. For the librarian a book is an atom, while for the printer—let alone the writer—it is very much a composite. But here we have to realize that what we are dealing with is not a matter of metaphysics or ontology but one of practical procedure. Be it in physics or in matters of language and cognition, atomicity is thus not an ontological but a practical and contextually purposive condition. It is not the sort of thread from which a metaphysical fabric can successfully be woven.

The upshot is that what we have to deal with in this context is a pragmatic shift based on the recognition of the centrality of a functional/purposive context of deliberation. In this or that purposive setting we may decide to *regard* something as atomic here and now—though we might well proceed quite differently in other contexts.

Clearly, however, any such functionalistic and thereby contextual construal of atomicity is totally at odds with the aspiration of those programs of metaphysical atomism. Any deconstruction compositional of simplicity as something that is both respectival and nonabsolute (inevitably comparative) is going to be incompatible with the aspirations of process atomism, logical atomism, cognitive atomism, and action-theoretical atomism. Accordingly, all of these programs of atomistic metaphysics have become unraveled through their demand for decompositional ultimacy by way of absolutely simpler processes, statements, facts, actions, or whatever, all of which have proven as insubstantial as the smile of the Cheshire cat.[17]

Cognition Is Not Summative

So much, then, for the atomistic summativity of existence as such. But what of the summativity of existence explanations? For the question posed in the first section of this chapter can be reformulated by asking if existence explanation is mereologically summative in nature—if explaining the existence of the part will thereby explain the existence of the whole.

Cognition, of course, is not mereologically summative. Understanding each step of an argument does not ensure understanding the argument itself: to comprehend each sentence of the text is not necessarily to comprehend the text as a whole. And so, even as the existence of a whole involves more than that of its parts, so knowing or explaining the existence of a whole involves more than knowing or explaining the existence of its parts. Accordingly, explaining the existence of a structured whole is not simply to explain the existence of its several parts but also to require explaining them being organized and structured in the particular way at issue with that whole. Only when dealing with an unstructured aggregate—a mere set or collection of unrelated objects—does the existence of the parts automatically assure that of the whole.

The Hume-Edwards thesis can be construed in two rather different ways. One is that a whole needs no existence explanation over and above the distributive existence explanations of its parts. The other is that the whole *admits* no existence explanation over and above the distributive existence explanations of its parts. But in both versions alike, the thesis is rendered unworkable by the circumstance that any structural whole is something over and above the mere collectivity of its constituent parts.

With totally unstructured wholes—such as various sets at issue in abstract mathematics—the Hume-Edwards thesis no doubt obtains. (And this might explain why Bertrand Russell was drawn to it, seeing that mere sets are structureless as such.)[18] But of course with any whole that is concrete rather than abstract, this situation will simply not obtain.

Interestingly, the *converse* of the failed thesis of explanatory summativity does obtain—but only in a qualified format. For we do have it that

> If a whole exists, then all of its essential (existence-requisite) parts do.

But naturally this version of the principle obtains only once the matter has been "adjusted" by that trivializing reference to *essential* parts, which dismisses from purview the redundant, dispensable, superfluous parts that might possibly—or even normally—belong to wholes of a certain sort. To be sure, for a whole to exist *as it is* those parts must be there *as they are,* where this encompasses whatever relationships in fact obtain among them. But this does no more than to implement the idea that a change in one or more of its parts is the basis for imputing a change to the whole. And here the converse obtains as well. For if those parts all exist *as they do* (and thereby in their actually prevailing interrelationships), the whole must also exists *as it does*. But the recourse to that "as is" terminology which is crucial for these claims effectively trivializes the matter.

In general, then, explaining the existence of these parts (matters of interrelationship left aside) does nothing to explain the existence of any whole in which the interrelationship of those parts plays a significant role.

Review

And so in the Hume-Leibniz controversy regarding the summativity of existence explanation, it is clear that Leibniz was right. For the universe is a *cosmos*—an ordered structure of components and occurrences. And it explains that the existence and composition of these constituents separately and distributively does not account for their structure of interrelationship collectively and conjointly in the way that would explain the existence of the universe as it is. It does not get at the principles of order and arrangement that make the resulting whole into a cosmos—a single, all-embracing, coherent manifold with its characteristic body of coordinative laws and principles.

To be sure, it might well be objected that it is exactly these laws and principles that we deploy in our explanation of the world's things and events, and that thereby the resources adequate for a distributive existence explanation will also afford the materials for accommodating the structural features needed to account for the whole. And in a way this is quite true. But it still leaves open a large explanatory gap that was seized upon and emphasized by Leibniz himself. For though we here involve and use the laws and principles that characterize nature's modus operandi, we do not manage to explain them. To explain adequately the existence of the world as is we must not just provide explanations for its constituent things and occurrences, but for its laws as well. We must, that is, have an answer to the question of why the laws of nature that fix the modus operandi of this world as it is are as they are. And this is an aspect of collective reality that no distributive explanation of its constituents manages to address—let alone resolve.

Critics of the cosmological argument for God's role in nature have projected one sort of objection to the need for a transcendental (world-exceeding) explanation of the natural world by arguing as follows:

> The world of nature consists of nothing other than its particular constituent concrete things and occurrences. If we can account for each of them (as we indeed can—at least in theory—on the basis of natural science's facts and laws) then (by summation)

> we have accounted for the whole. No further and
> deeper principle is required.[19]

But clearly there is a problem here, because nothing assures that premise that "Nature as a whole is nothing other than its particular constituent concrete things and events." For nature is—or must be assumed to be— a *structured* whole. And we have not accounted for nature so conceived unless we have explained its structure as well—that is, in effect, have explored why it is that nature's laws are as they are. And this, as Leibniz emphatically insisted, is a project whose accomplishment requires some further facts or principles than what is required to account for nature's several constituent components. To be sure, this principle need not be transcendental (that is nature-external or nature-exceeding). But it does, at the very least, seem to require some deeper principles of order then those that merely explain nature's components and occurrences.

Thus consider one philosopher's claim that "If all events in nature do have causes, that does not entitle us to demand a *non-natural* course for nature as a whole."[20] Of course, use of that qualifier "non-natural" in place of "further" or "deeper" unduly prejudices the issue. But even after this needed corrigendum, the thesis at issue is still profoundly questionable, exactly for the reason we have been canvassing; to wit, that accounting for its parts is not necessarily to account adequately for a structured whole.

Metaphysics, in sum, is an unavoidably complex business: its problems cannot be managed adequately by prizing its objects apart into a more elemental comments. Structures, interrelationships, and inter- connections are crucial here. Accordingly, the achievement of adequacy in their domain demands an approach that cannot proceed piecemeal: our approach must be holistic and systemic if we are to succeed in deal- ing adequately with the inherent complexities of the issues.

Externalities and Negative Side Effects

Economists characterize as "externalities" the costs that a given agent's operations engender for other participants in the economic system—the expenditures that one agent's activities exact from other agents, whether willingly or unwillingly. They are the operating costs that an agent simply off-loads onto the wider community, the expenses that one generates for others in the course of addressing one's own im- mediate concerns—as for example, when a farmer's fertilizers contami- nate the drinking water of his neighbors. It is interesting to observe that substantially the same phenomenon can arise also in philosophy. For in philosophy we may, in solving a problem within some particular domain, create major difficulties for the solution of problems elsewhere, even in areas seemingly far removed from the original issue. It is instructive to consider some examples of this phenomenon.

Example 1: Epistemology and Ethics. Suppose that we are sailing on the open sea on a vacation cruise ship. It is dusk, and the visibility is getting poor. As we stroll on deck along the rail of the ship, there is suddenly a shout, "Man overboard!" Someone grabs a life preserver from the nearby bulkhead and rushes with it toward the railing. Suddenly, he comes to a stop and hesitates a moment. To our astonishment, he turns, retraces his steps, and replaces the life preserver, calmly proceeding step-by-step as the place the men fell in gets farther away, then disappears. Puzzled and chagrined, we turn to the individual and ask why he broke off the rescue attempt. The response runs as follows: "Of course, throwing that life preserver was my first instinct, as my behavior clearly showed. But then some ideas from my undergraduate epistemology courses came to mind and convinced me that it made no sense to continue." Intrigued, we ask for more details and receive the following response:

> Consider what we actually knew. All we could see was that something that looked like a human head was bobbing out there in the water. But the visibility was poor. It could have been an old mop or a lady's wig stand. Those noises we took for distant shouts could well have been no more than a pulsing of the engines and the howling of the wind. There was simply no decisive evidence that it was actually a person out there. And then I remembered William Kingdon Clifford's classic dictum: "It is wrong always, everywhere, and for anyone, to believe anything upon insufficient evidence." So why act on a belief that there was actually a human being in danger out there, when the evidence for any such belief was clearly insufficient? And why carry out a rescue attempt when you do not accept that someone actually needs rescuing?

Something has clearly gone badly wrong here. We may not choose to fault our misguided shipmate as an epistemologist, yet we cannot but wonder about his moral competency.

Even if I unhesitatingly accept and endorse the abstract principle that one must try to be helpful to others in situations of need, I am clearly in moral difficulty if I operate on too stringent a standard of evidence in relevant contexts—if, for example, I allow skeptical concerns about other minds to paralyze me from ever recognizing another creature as a human person. For then I will be far-reachingly precluded from doing things that, morally considered, I *ought* to do. William James rightly noted this connection between epistemology and morality, in insisting that the skeptic rudely treads morality underfoot: "If I refuse to stop a murder because I am in [some] doubt whether it is not justifiable homicide, I am virtually abetting the crime. If I refuse to bale out a boat because I am in doubt whether my effort will keep her afloat, I am really helping to sink her. . . . Scepticism in moral matters is an active ally of immorality."[21] There is much to be said for this view of the matter.

To operate in life with *epistemological* principles so stringent as to impede the discharge of one's standard *moral* obligations is to invite justified reproach. Where the interests of others are at risk, we cannot, with moral appropriateness, deploy evidential standards of acceptability of a higher, more demanding sort than those that are normally operative in the community in the ordinary run of cases. At this point, epistemology has moral ramifications. For morality as we know it requires a common-sense, down-to-earth epistemology for its appropriate implementation.

In such a case, then, the stance we take in one domain (epistemology) has significant repercussions for the way we can proceed in another (ethics). The issues arising in these seemingly remote areas stand in systemic interlinkage. Externalities can come into play. A problem-solution that looks like a bargain in the one domain may exact an unacceptable price in the other.

Example 2: Semantics and Metaphysics. For another illustration—one of a rather different sort—consider the semantical position urged by a contemporary Oxford philosopher who maintains that there are no incognizable facts, because there actually is a fact of the matter only when a claim to this effect is such that "we [humans] could in a finite time bring ourselves into a position in which we were [fully] justified either in asserting or in denying [the contention at issue]."[22] This sort of "finite decidability semantics" holds that a proposition is communicatively meaningful—qualifies as inherently true or false—only if the matter can actually be settled, decisively and conclusively, one way or the other, by a finite effort in a limited time.

But this doctrinal path issuing from semantics leads to some strange destinations. For it automatically precludes the prospect of maintaining anything like our commonsense view of things in the world about us. In this way, the wolf of a highly problematic metaphysic comes concealed in the sheep's clothing of innocuous-looking semantical theory.

For consider: as we standardly think about things within the conceptual framework of our fact-oriented thought and discourse, *any* real physical object has more facets than it will (or indeed can) ever actually manifest in experience. Every objective property of a real thing has consequences of a dispositional nature, and these are never actually surveyable in toto, seeing that the dispositions that particular concrete things inevitably have endow them with an infinite aspect that cannot be comprehended within experience. This desk, for example, has a limitless manifold of phenomenal features of the type "having a certain appearance from a particular point of view." It is perfectly clear that most of these will never be actualized in experience. Moreover, a thing *is* what it *does*: to be a desk or an apple is to behave like one. Entity and lawfulness are coordinated correlates—a good Kantian point.[23] And this fact that things as such involve lawful comportment means that the finitude of experience precludes any prospect of the *exhaustive* manifestation of the descriptive facets of any real thing. Some of the ramifications of this circumstance deserve closer attention.

Physical objects, as we standardly conceive them, not only have more properties than they ever *will* overtly manifest, but also actually have more than they *could* ever actually manifest, because the dispositional properties of things always involve what might be characterized as mutually preemptive conditions of realization. A cube of sugar, for example, has the dispositional property of reacting in a particular way if subjected to a temperature of $10,000°$ C and of reacting in a certain way if placed for one hundred hours in a large, turbulent body of water. But if either of these conditions is ever realized, it will destroy the lump of sugar as a lump of sugar, and thus block the prospect of its ever bringing the other property to manifestation. Because of such inherent conflicts, the severally possible realization of various dispositions can fail to be conjointly compossible, and so the dispositional properties of a thing cannot ever be manifest in toto—not just in practice but in principle.

On the other hand, to say of the apple that its only features are those it actually manifests is to run afoul of our conception of an apple. For to deny—or even merely to refuse to be committed to—the claim that it *would* manifest particular features *if* certain conditions came about (for example, that it would have such-and-such a taste if eaten) is to be driven to withdrawing the claim that it is an apple. A real thing is always conceptualized as having features that transcend our actual experience of it. All discourse about objective things involves an element of *experience-transcending imputation*—of commitment to claims that go beyond the experientially acquirable information, but yet claims whose rejection would mean our having to withdraw the thing-characterization at issue. To say of something that it is an apple or a stone or a tree is to become inexorably committed to claims about it that go beyond the data we have—and even beyond those that we can, in the nature of things, ever actually acquire. Real things always do and must have features that transcend our determinable knowledge of them.

In the light of such considerations, it emerges that a finite decidability semantics—though seemingly a merely linguistic doctrine about meaningful assertion—is in fact not just theory of language or logic. For it now has major repercussions in very different domains. In particular, it has the far-reaching metaphysical consequence of precluding any prospect of the commonsense realism at issue in our standard conception of the world's things. On its basis, any statement of objective fact—however modest and commonsensical—is immediately rendered meaningless by the infinitude of its evidential ramifications. Thus, a "merely semantical" doctrine seemingly devised to serve the interests of a philosophy of language has implications that preempt a major substantive position in metaphysics.

Its conflict with the commonsense realism of ordinary discourse does not, of course, demonstrate that finite decidability semantics is ultimately incorrect. But it once again illustrates vividly the ramified interconnectedness of philosophical doctrines—the fact that a seemingly attractive problem-solution in one area may be available as such only at the cost of creating massive problems elsewhere. The theory is certainly one that we cannot reasonably accept on its local, semantical recommendations alone, irrespective of wider implications. Externalities are once again at work.

ৡ

Other illustrations are readily available. A metaphysical determinism that negates free will runs afoul of a traditionalistic ethical theory that presupposes it. A philosophical anthropology that takes human life to originate at conception clashes with a social philosophy that sees abortion as morally unproblematic. A theory of rights that locates all responsibility in the contractual reciprocity of freely consenting parties creates problems for a morality of concern for animals. And the list goes on and on.

The basic reason why philosophical issues are interrelated across different subject-matter domains lies in their aporetic nature—their invariable linkage to the situation where we confront groups of propositions that may seem individually plausible but are collectively inconsistent. For as was indicated above, the data of philosophy—the manifold of nontrivially evidentiated considerations with which it must come to terms—is always such that internal tensions and inconsistencies arise within it. The range of contentions that there is *some* reason to accept here outrun the range of what *can* be maintained in the light of consistency considerations. And the diversity of participants in such a conflict of overextension is almost always such as to outrun the boundaries of the thematic and disciplinary units that we generally entertain.

Systematic Interconnectedness as a Consequence of Aporetic Complexity

The aporetic perspective on philosophical issues puts the phenomenon of philosophical externalities into sharp relief. It shows that philosophical doctrines are inextricably interconnected, spreading their implications across the frontiers of very different areas disjoint in subject matter. The ramifications and implications of philosophical contentions do not respect the discipline's taxonomic boundaries.

The examples we have been considering thus convey a clear lesson. We all too easily risk losing sight of this interconnectedness when we ride our hobbyhorses in pursuit of the technicalities of a limited subdomain. In actuality, the stance we take on questions in one domain will generally have substantial implications and ramification for very different issues in other seemingly distant domains. And exactly this is why systematization is so important in philosophy—because the way we *do* answer some questions will have limiting repercussions for the way we *can* answer others. We cannot divide our philosophical convictions into conveniently separated compartments in the comfortable expectation that what we maintain in one area of the field will have no unwelcome implications for what we are inclined to maintain in others.

The long and short of it is that the realm of truth is unified, and its components are interlinked. Change your mind regarding one fact about the real, and you cannot leave all the rest unaffected. To qualify as adequate, one's account of things must be a systemic whole whose components are interrelated by relation of systemic interaction or feedback.

In the final analysis, philosophy is a system, because it is concerned to indicate, or at least to *estimate*, the truth about things, and "the truth about reality" is a system.[24] Its various sectors and components are bound to dovetail smoothly with one another. For even if one is reluctant to claim that *reality* as such must be systematic, the fact remains that an adequate *account* of it must surely be so. Even as we must take a sober view of inebriation, so we must aim at a coherent account of even an incoherent world. Philosophy's commitment to the project of rational inquiry, to the task of making coherent and comprehensive sense of things, means that an adequate philosophy must be holistic, accommodating and coordinating all aspects of its concerns in a single unified and coherent whole, with the result that any viable philosophical doctrine will and can be no more than a particular piece fitting smoothly into the wider puzzle.

Moreover, in philosophy, there are no secure axioms—no starter set of absolutely certain "givens" whose implications we can follow through without question to the bitter end. In general, we cannot assess the acceptability of our contentions solely in terms of the security of their antecedents, but must reassess their acceptability in the light of their consequences and not only locally but globally. The implicit interconnectedness of philosophical issues means that the price philosophers must pay for overly narrow specialization—for confining attention narrowly to one particular set of issues—is compromising the tenability of their position.

Insofar as such a perspective is right, it emerges that the range of relevant consequences cannot be confined to the local area of the immediate thematic environs of the contention, but will have to involve its more remote reverberations as well. If an otherwise appealing contention in semantics wreaks havoc in metaphysics or in the philosophy of mathematics, that too will have to be weighed when the question of its tenability arises. The absolute idealist for whom "time is unreal" cannot appropriately just write off the ethicist's interest in future eventuations (as regards, for example, the situation that will obtain when the time to make good a promise arrives) or the political philosopher's concern for the well-being future generations. The materialist cannot simply dismiss the boundary-line issues involved in the moral question of why pointlessly to damage a computer one owns is simply foolish, but pointlessly to injure an animal is outright wicked.

The crux is that philosophical issues are organically interconnected. Positions that maximize local advantages may fail to be optimal from a global point of view. In the final analysis, only positions that are *holistically* adequate can be deemed to be really satisfactory.

From Greek antiquity to the nineteenth century, a conviction prevailed that the branches of philosophy could be arranged in a neat hierarchy of sequential dependence and fundamentality, somewhat along the lines of logic, epistemology, metaphysics, ethics (axiology), and politico-social philosophy. In fact, however, the various subdomains of philosophy are interlinked by a complex network of reciprocal interrelationships. (For example, one needs epistemology to validate principles of logic, and yet one must use logic for reasoning in epistemology.) Justificatory argumentation in philosophy admits of no neat Aristotelian order of prior/posterior in its involvement with the subject's components. The inherent interrelationships of the issues is such that we have no alternative but to see the sectors of philosophy as interconnected through interlocking cycles that bind the subject's various branches into one systematic whole.

Because its issues are interrelated, philosophical argumentation must look not just to antecedents but to consequences as well. Virtually nothing of philosophical relevancy is beyond question and altogether immune to criticism and possible rejection. Pretty much everything is potentially at risk. All of the "data" of philosophy are defeasible—anything might in the final analysis have to be abandoned, whatever its source: science, common sense, common knowledge. One recent theorist writes: "No philosophical, or any other, theory can provide a view which violates common sense and remain logically consistent. For the truth of common sense is assumed by all theories. . . . This necessity to conform to common sense establishes a constraint upon the interpretations philosophical theories can offer."[25] But this overstates the case. The philosophical landscape is littered with theories that tread common sense underfoot. As philosophy goes about its work of rendering our beliefs coherent, something to which we are deeply attached often has to give somewhere along the line, and we can never say at the outset where the blow will or will not fall. Systemic considerations may well in the end lead our most solid-seeming suppositions into insuperable difficulty—as also can happen in the context of natural science. And the only cure for failures of systematization in philosophy lies in the construction of better systems.

Chapter 6

The Structure of
Philosophical Dialectic

Philosophical Aporetics

To be sure, Aristotle was right in saying that philosophy begins in wonder and that securing answers to our questions is the aim of the enterprise. But of course we do not just want answers but coherent answers, seeing that these alone have a chance of being collectively true. The quest for consistency is an indispensable part of the quest for truth. The quest for consistency is one of the driving dynamic forces of philosophy.

But the cruel fact is that theorizing itself yields contradictory results. In moving from empirical observation to philosophical theorizing, we do not leave contradiction behind—it continues to dog our footsteps. And just as reason must correct sensation, so more-refined and more-elaborate reason is always needed as a corrective for less-refined and less-elaborate reason. The source of contradiction is not just in the domain of sensation but in that of reasoned reflection as well. We are not just *led into* philosophy by the urge to consistency, we are ultimately *kept* at it by this same urge.

In philosophy we constantly confront the painful fact that what we deem to be rules have their exceptions. And the search for conceptual distinctions to implement the needed qualifications is never ending. William James wrote: "Things are 'with' one another in many ways, but nothing includes everything or dominates over everything. The word 'and' trails along after every sentence. Something always escapes."[1] But this does not go far enough. While "and" may trail along after every sentence, in philosophy "but" trails along after every paragraph. The job of elaboration is never quite finished. The difficulties we resolve at one point through seemingly helpful "clarifications" burst out again at another. No formulation of a position can dispel all the problems, answer all the questions, resolve all the difficulties. Inconsistency keeps breaking in upon us.

To restore consistency among incompatible beliefs calls for abandoning some of them as they stand. In general, however, philosophers do not provide for consistency-restoration wholly by way of rejection. Rather, they have recourse to *modification*, replacing the abandoned belief with a duly qualified revision thereof. Since (by hypothesis) each thesis belonging to an aporetic cluster is individually attractive, simple rejection lets the case for the rejected thesis go unacknowledged. Only by modifying the thesis through a resort to distinctions can one manage to give proper recognition to the full range of considerations that initially led into aporetic difficulty. Confronted with an aporetic cluster of collectively incompatible commitments, we naturally want to eliminate the inconsistency in which we have become enmeshed. Consistency is the most elemental demand of philosophical rationality—its lack would compromise the entire project as a cognitive endeavor.

But how can one eliminate inconsistency? In essentials, the answer is simple. One can always restore consistency among incompatible commitments by abandoning some of the beliefs that engender the difficulty. Inconsistency results from overcommitment, and we can avoid it by curtailing our commitments.

Consider, for example, that sector of seventeenth-century metaphysics that revolved about the following aporetic cluster:

1. Extension is substantial (in constituting material *res extensa*).
2. Thought is substantial (in constituting immaterial *res cogitans*).
3. Thought and extension are coordinate items that have the same standing and status.
4. Substance as such is uniform: at bottom it has but one type and is a genus of one single species.

Clearly, these contentions are mutually incompatible. The inconsistency can, of course, be removed by deletions, and this is obviously the way to go. But as always, the weeding out needed to restore consistency can be accomplished in different ways. The following alternatives are open:

- Abandon (1) and (3): Idealism of a type that regards extended matter as merely phenomenal (Leibniz and Berkeley).
- Abandon (2) and (3): Materialism in the form of a theory that sees thought as the causal product of the operations of matter (Gassendi and Hobbes).
- Abandon (1) and (2): Metaphysical aspectivalism and, in particular, a theory that takes both thought and material extension to be mere attributes of a single, all-encompassing substance (Spinoza).
- Abandon (4): Thought/matter dualism (Descartes).

All of these exits from inconsistency were available, and all were in fact used by one or another thinker of the period.

Consider another example. Pre-Socratic philosophizing was involved in coming to terms with the following family of mutually incompatible beliefs:

1. There is such a thing as physical change.
2. Something persists unaffected throughout physical change.
3. Matter does not persist unaffected through physical change.
4. Matter (in its various guises) is all there is.

There are four ways out of the inconsistency generated by these theses:

- Deny 1: Change is a mere illusion (Zeno and Parmenides).
- Deny 2: Nothing whatever persists unaffected through physical change (Heraclitus—*panta rhei*).
- Deny 3: Matter does indeed persist unaffected throughout physical change, albeit only *in the small*—in its "atoms" (the atomists).
- Deny 4: Matter is not all there is. There is also *"mathematical form,"* with physical change being at bottom a matter of alteration in geometric structure (Pythagoras) or in arithmetical proportion (Anaxagoras).

To free ourselves from the grasp of aporetic inconsistency, we must jettison some of the theses that have enmeshed us in difficulty. There will always be different alternatives here, so that a choice among them is possible and necessary.

The Role of Distinctions

Distinctions enable the philosopher to remove inconsistencies not just by the brute negativism of thesis *rejection* but by the more subtle and constructive device of thesis *qualification*. The crux of a distinction is not mere negation or denial, but the amendment of an untenable thesis into something positive that does the job better. By way of example, consider the following aporetic cluster:

1. All events are caused.
2. If an action issues from free choice, then it is causally unconstrained.
3. Free will exists—people can and do make and act upon free choices.

Clearly, one way to exit from inconsistency is to abandon thesis (2). We might well, however, do this not by way of outright abandonment but rather by speaking of the "causally unconstrained" in Spinoza's sense of *externally* originating casualty. For consider the result of deploying a distinction that divides the second premise into two parts:

2.1 Actions based on free choice are unconstrained by *external* causes.
2.2 Actions based on free choice are unconstrained by *internal* causes.

Once (2) is so divided, the initial inconsistent triad (1)–(3) give way to the quartet (1), (2.1), (2.2), (3). But we can resolve *this* aporetic cluster by rejecting (2.2) while yet retaining (2.1)—thus, in effect, *replacing* (2) by a weakened version. Such recourse to a distinction—here that between internal and external causes—makes it possible to avert the aporetic inconsistency and does so in a way that minimally disrupts the plausibility situation.

To examine the workings of this sort of process somewhat further, consider an aporetic cluster that set the stage for various theories of early Greek philosophy:

1. Reality is one (homogeneous).
2. Matter is real.
3. Form is real.
4. Matter and form are distinct sorts of things (heterogeneous).

In looking for a resolution here, one might consider rejecting (2). This could be done, however, not by simply *abandoning* it, but rather by *replacing* it—on the idealistic precedent of Zeno and Plato—with something along the following lines:

> 2'. Matter is not real as an independent mode of existence; rather it is merely quasi real, a mere *phenomenon*, an appearance somehow grounded in immaterial reality.

The new quartet (1), (2'), (3), (4) is entirely cotenable.

Now, in adopting this resolution, one again resorts to a *distinction*—namely, that between

> a. Strict reality as self-sufficiently independent existence

and

> b. Derivative or attenuated reality as a (merely phenomenal) product of the operation of the unqualifiedly real.

Use of such a distinction between unqualified and phenomenal reality makes it possible to resolve an aporetic cluster—yet not by simply *abandoning* one of those paradox-engendering theses but rather by *qualifying* it. Note, however, that once we follow Zeno and Plato in replacing (2) by (2')—and accordingly reinterpret matter as representing a "mere phenomenon"—the substance of thesis (4) is profoundly altered; the old contention can still be maintained, but it now gains a new significance in the light of new distinctions.

One might—alternatively—abandon thesis (3). However, one would then presumably not simply adopt "form is not real" but rather would go over to the qualified contention that "form is not *independently* real; it is no more than a transitory (changeable) state of matter." And this can be looked at the other way around, as saying "form *is* (in a way) real, although only insofar as it is taken to be no more than a transitory state of matter." This, in effect, would be the position of the atomists, who incline to see as implausible any recourse to mechanisms outside the realm of the material.

Aporetic inconsistency can always be resolved in this way; we can always "save the phenomena"—that is, retain the crucial core of our various beliefs in the face of apparent consideration—by introducing suitable distinctions and qualifications. Once apory breaks out, we can thus salvage our philosophical commitments by *complicating* them, through revisions in the light of appropriate distinctions, rather than abandon them altogether.

To be sure, distinctions are not needed if *all* that concerns us is averting inconsistency; simple thesis abandonment, mere refusal to assert, will suffice for that end. But distinctions are necessary if we are to maintain informative positions and provide answers to our questions. We can guard against inconsistency by avoiding commitment. But such skeptical refrainings leave us empty-handed. Distinctions are the instruments we use in the (potentially never-ending) work of rescuing our assertoric commitments from inconsistency while yet salvaging what we can.

The history of philosophy is shot through with distinctions introduced to avert aporetic difficulties. Already in the dialogues of Plato, the first systematic writings in philosophy, we encounter distinctions at every turn. In book 1 of the *Republic*, for example, Socrates' interlocutor quickly falls into the following apory:

1. Rational people always pursue their own interests.
2. Nothing that is in a person's interest can be disadvantageous to him.
3. Even rational people sometimes do things that prove disadvantageous.

Here, inconsistency is averted by distinguishing between two senses of the "interests" of a person—namely, what is *actually* advantageous to him and what he merely *thinks* to be so (that is, between *real* and *seeming* interests). Again, in the discussion of "nonbeing" in the *Sophist*, the Eleatic stranger entraps Theaetetus in an inconsistency from which he endeavors to extricate himself by distinguishing between "nonbeing" in the sense of not existing *at all* and in the sense of not existing *in a certain mode*. For the most part, the Platonic dialogues present a dramatic unfolding of one distinction after another.

And this situation is typical in philosophy. The natural dialectic of problem-solving here drives us even more deeply into drawing distinctions, so as to bring new, more sophisticated concepts upon the scene.

Whenever a particular aporetic thesis is rejected, the optimal course is not to abandon it altogether, but rather to minimize the loss by introducing a distinction by whose aid it may be retained *in part*. After all, we do have some commitment to the data that we reject, and are committed to saving as much as we can. (This, of course, is implicit in our treating those data as such in the first place.)

A distinction accordingly reflects a *concession*, an acknowledgment of some element of acceptability in the thesis that is being rejected. However, distinctions always bring a new concept upon the stage of consideration and thus put a new topic on the agenda. And they thereby present invitations to carry the discussion further, opening up new issues that were heretofore inaccessible. Distinctions are the doors through which philosophy moves on to new questions and problems. They bring new concepts and new theses to the fore.

The unfolding of distinctions accordingly plays a key role in philosophical inquiry because new concepts crop up in their wake so as to open up new territory for reflection. In the course of philosophy's dialectical development, new concepts and new theses come constantly to the fore and operate so as to open up new issues. And so in securing answers to our old questions we come to confront new questions that could not even be asked before.

In philosophy there is an ever-renewed need for further refinements and extensions. We arrive at the fundamental law of philosophical development: *Any given philosophical position, at any particular stage in its development, will, if developed further, encounter inconsistencies.* No formulation of a philosophical position can ever be fully adequate— definitive finality is destined always to elude us.

As the thought of a philosopher becomes fully elaborated— as its conceptual mechanisms are refined and extended and clarified by himself, by his followers, or by his "school"—his position's inner tensions come to light within the overall set of its commitments. Trouble breaks out within the overall sys tem in the form of aporetic inconsistency among the things we deem plausible; further difficulties always arise; additional qualifications and refinements are always needed.

The Structure of Dialectic

Dialectic has traditionally moved along tracks initially sketched out by Aristotle.[2] And philosophical dialectic in specific has a nine-part structure much along the lines initially envisioned by Hegel.[3] At the outset there is a thesis that is predicated on a descriptive assimilation or analogy. And then the first stage of deliberations has three parts.

Stage 1

1.1   Thesis (Positive analogy or assimilation)
    Example: Human actions are free.

1.2   Antitheses (Contrary denial of the thesis)
    Example: Human actions are causally necessitated.

1.3   Synthesis (Distinction-based reconciliation of the thesis and others).
    Example: We must distinguish between voluntary and involuntary human acts. The voluntary ones are free, the involuntary causally necessitated.

At the next step we move on to the duly revised and qualified version of the case.

Stage 2

2.1   Revised and qualified thesis
    Example: Voluntary human actions are free.

2.2   Revised and qualified antithesis
    Example: Involuntary human actions are causally necessitated.

2.3   Second-order synthesis
    Example: There are other forms of constraint over and above causal necessitation—for example, duress or undue influence.

At the third stage of analysis we have a second-level explanation or commentary on the shifts effected at the prior stages, as per

Stage 3

3.1   Explanation/commentary on the move from 1.1 to 2.1
    Example: Explanation/commentary on why and how volition impacts on free agency

3.2   Explanation/commentary on the move from 1.2 to 2.2
    Example: Explanation/commentary on why and how causal necessitation impacts on involuntariness

3.3   Explanation/commentary on the move from 1.3 to 2.3
    Example: Explanation/commentary on why and how voluntary/involuntary and causally necessitated/genuinely contingent are interrelated

Figure 6.1
Philosophical Dialectics

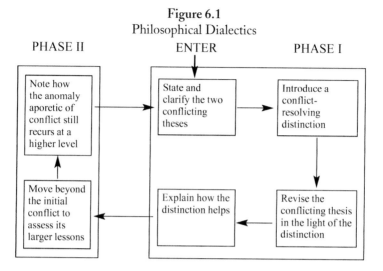

The overall process at issue can be represented pictorially by the flow diagram of fig. 6.1. The development of a philosophical position is accordingly a potentially never-ending task that takes on the form of a dialectical cycle. In philosophy, we can never manage to complete matters by reaching a definitive stopping point at which *everything* that needs to be said has been accomplished. No doubt the situation is worst at first. It is an objection standardly cast against a new philosophical contention that it is "unclear"—and so it is bound to be until its implications and ramifications get worked out. But the development of a philosophical position always remains to some extent problematic. The difficulties become displaced but not annihilated. At any and every stage we have no more than a rough, imperfectly developed project on which further work needs to be done by way of overcoming difficulties and removing inexactnesses.

And so the development of a philosophical position moves from a level of relative accessibility (elementality, fundamentality) to one of increasing technicality (elaborateness, sophistication) in the manner indicated in fig. 6.2. The system be comes rearticulated and reformulated in a way that is ever more ramified and complex.

Philosophizing is, as it were, a dialectical game that gets played at different levels of difficulty in the course of time. When one examines the historical development of a philosophical position, one can always discern the unfolding of its inner perplexities—those crisis junctures at which it slips into inconsistency. It is this ultimate encounter with inconsistency within "established" philosophical positions that makes for

Figure 6.2
The Dialectical Cycle of Philosophical Complexification

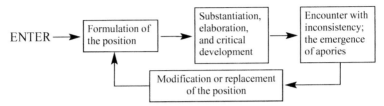

inherent instability and provides the dynamical impetus to the ongoing alteration or replacement of philosophical systems.

Our philosophical questions are always answered incompletely, in ways that inevitably leave further crucial detail to be supplied. Philosophy moves inexorably into increasing technicality and sophistication. And this makes interested bystanders impatient. They cry, "Will philosophy ever again address the heavens? Will it contribute anything to man's vision, rather than merely clarifying it?"[4] But this sort of complaint about enmeshment in technicalities overlooks the filiation of means and ends in question resolution that links the technical issues of philosophy to the fundamental presystemic questions from which they arise. We are driven to those technical microissues by the inexorable necessity of addressing them in order to secure rationally adequate resolutions of the presystemic macroissues afforded by "eternal problems" of philosophy.

The answers we give to philosophical questions are always only rough and approximate. Our solutions to philosophical problems engender further problems. They are always open to challenges that require additional elaboration and refinement. In philosophy we are always impelled toward greater sophistication—our problem-solving distinctions always bring yet further distinctions. We are led to com pound wheels upon wheels—adding further epicycles of complexity to the theories we are seeking to render acceptable. But inconsistency-averting elaboration at one point only engenders further difficulties at another. No articulation of a philosophical system is free from problems.

Developmental Dialectics

A dialectical process of Hegelian proportions is at work. According to Hegel, it is the essential character of human reason to involve itself in, contradictions—conflicts of commitment that it first posits but then overcomes through an eventual reconciliation at a higher level. The philosopher who analyzed this aspect of the history of the subject most clearly was Johann Friedrich Herbart. He proposed that the history of philosophy should be recast in issue-oriented form and should in fact be written in terms of the development of doctrines devised to resolve successively encountered antinomies along the general lines of fig. 6.3. The history of philosophy, he held, should be written as a history of problems (and thus in a genre of which, even today, we have but a few fragmentary samples).

Herbart maintained that the experiential concepts in whose terms we represent and process our cognitive experiences in science and ordinary life always involve internal conflicts. An experiential concept A unites two disparate elements, M and N, that do not stand in a logico-conceptual union but are united by a strictly factual bond. There is a tension or contradiction here. We can neither (on theoretical grounds) maintain that there is a fusion of M and N in A, nor yet (on factual grounds) can we deny this connection outright. Logic rejects the conceptual fusing of M and N. Experience rejects their separation. All we can do is suppose that there is some new element, some distinction that splits M into M_1 and M_2, one which is rigidly joined to N, the other strictly distinct from it At best, then, we can see A as an unstable compound, oscillating between A_1 (where M_1 is problematically conjoined with N) and A_2 (where M_2 is unproblematically disjoined from N). Accordingly, every experiential concept is the ground from which some suitable "supplementary concept must emerge to yield a distinction capable of restoring consistency.

Herbart saw the prime task of philosophy as the reworking of our experiential concepts so as to restore consistency—to effect an integration that relegates these inner contradictions to the realm of mere appearance. Philosophy strives to overcome the internal inconsistency of

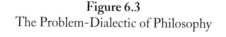

Figure 6.3
The Problem-Dialectic of Philosophy

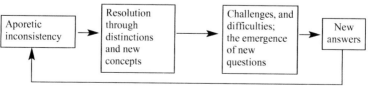

our presystemic concepts. Throughout our philosophizing, those experiential concepts will inevitably come to be transcended by successors who seek to resolve the tensions of their presystemic predecessors. This process, Herbart's "method of relations" (*Methode der Beziehungen*), is the counterpart in his system of the Hegelian dialectic. As Wilhelm Dilthey put it:

> Herbart was the first who regressed analytically from the course of philosophical development to the particular problems that were the prime mover in the minds of individual thinkers. For him, philosophy was "the systematic study (*Wissenschaft*) of philosophical questions and problems." And so he responded to the question of the nature of philosophizing with the reply that it is "the endeavor to solve problems." In the first redaction of his *Introduction to Philosophy*, he places the motive force to philosophizing in the puzzles and contradictions regarding the nature of things. Our trying to put the pieces together, to see the world whole, occasions our initial discovery of philosophical problems.[5]

Herbert Spencer's law of development from indefinite homogeneity to more definite heterogeneity may not hold for biological development, but it certainly does hold for philosophical evolution. There is an ongoing exfoliation of more complex and internally diversified theories—an unfolding on whose course the aporetic theses at issue become increasingly refined and nuanced by means of successive distinctions. In philosophy, old doctrines never die, they just take on new guises. They become increasingly complex and sophisticated to meet the demands of new conditions and circumstances. In the course of the dialectical progress of philosophical development, more complex questions, more refined concepts, and more subtle distinctions are constantly introduced. There is not only increasing sophistication in conceptual machinery but also an ongoing expansion of the problem horizon of the particular doctrine at issue as new theories are introduced to resolve the aporetic inconsistencies of prior commitments.

To overcome the inconsistencies that arise at any given level of philosophical development, we must push on to the next, introducing more distinctions, more refinements, more detail and sophistication. We encounter here a key aspect of the developmental dynamics of philosophy: the impetus to the ever-continuing development and refinement of our philosophical positions. We are impelled to move ever further from the simpler presystemic issues that afford the starting point of our philosophical deliberations. (That is why philosophers nowadays are always much more comfortable in talking with colleagues about technical problems than in explaining to the plain man how these technical discussions bear on the big issues.) The history of philosophy consists largely in an ongoing confrontation between competing positions standing perpetually in conflict, though changing in detail through increasing sophistication and complexification.

In the general course of things, the dialectical unfolding of philosophical history presents a unified picture of treelike proportions. The tradition that develops a philosophical position lurches from one stage after another. At any given stage of development a theorist is in principle able to go back to a prior position and move forward along another path (*reculer pour mieux sauter*, as Leibniz liked to say). Moreover, one can also use "the wisdom of hindsight" to go back and introduce (as it were, ex post facto) new nodes at earlier junctures. Revisionism always affords an alternative to simple development. New and previously overlooked distinctions and refinements can be introduced at any stage.

This is why major philosophers are always driven back to making a fresh start. They have a penchant for "going back to square one" to create new paths out of (or *around*) old problems, and accordingly they view the inconclusiveness of earlier work with relish rather than dismay. Kant is typical in this regard when he writes in the *Prolegomena to Any Future Metaphysics*, "[M]y purpose is to persuade all those who think metaphysics worth studying that it is absolutely necessary to pause a moment . . . regarding all that has been done as undone."[6] The prospect of picking up the threads of earlier stages is ever present in philosophy—which explains why the history of the subject plays such an important role in its own development.

We arrive at a model of philosophical development that is essentially exfoliative. Every philosophical position is linked to and developmentally derived from a prior doctrine that contains its root idea. (In the realm of philosophical thought as in physical nature we have *ex nihilo nihil*.) This exfoliative process involves a superengrafting of new distinctions upon old, with new topics and issues continually emerging from our efforts to resolve prior problems. There is an unending process of introducing further elaborative refinement into the setting of old, preestablished views, an ongoing emergence of new positions to implement old doctrines. Thus, every philosophical concept and position always has a genealogy (an "archaeology," in currently fashionable terminology) that can trace back its origins programmatically through a means-end chain of problem-solving. Every position and distinction has its natural place in the developmental tree.

No one has stressed this aspect of philosophy more emphatically and eloquently than Dilthey: "Wholly in vain do various thinkers try to cast the whole past away in an endeavor to make a fresh start freed from all prejudgments. They cannot shake off what has been. The gods of the past come back uninvited to haunt them. The melody of our lives is inevitably sung to the accompanying voices of the past."[7] Nothing that belongs to the subject is wholly isolated or disconnected; the new is always part of an old, preestablished program. (Even Berkeleian immaterialism has its neoplatonic precursors.) And there is no reason of principle why the exfoliative process should ever stop.

The natural evolution of a philosophical school of thought is such that one always retains (some of) the old doctrines; it adheres to the old credos and formulas while constantly pouring new wine into the old bottles. The school is the "same" school because its key theses (though increasingly seen as extremely rough approximations) are still retained—its doctrinal allegiances (as opposed to its explanations) continue the same. It fights under the same old banners and celebrates the same old heroes. But the actual substance of its deliberations constantly changes through ongoing "refinement." (Often, indeed, the discussion wanders off into mere technicalities, with philosophers addressing issues that have evolved from issues that have evolved from issues, and so on, losing all sight of that crucial guiding thread of relevance needed to preserve a connection with the fundamental questions that gave the whole process its start.)

In philosophy we are thus faced with persisting schools of thought—ongoing traditions of doctrinal commitment in a continual state of inner development and mutual conflict. Such schools are united by agreement on first principles, but they are continually fragmented into subschools and sub-subschools through differentiation in matters of (increasingly subtle) detail. The process is one of a biological and evolutionary format with the development of genera, species, and ever more differentiated varieties. Things get increasingly complicated. Philosophizing is always a mixture of conservation and innovation—of preserving some element of a tradition while yet transforming it. Like it or not, even the most radical innovator in this field has some claim to the proud title of conservator, once applied honorifically to Jupiter and the Roman emperors. But this coin also has its other side.

In the long run, any given contribution to the dialectic of philosophical development will eventually become obsolete in the light of subsequent criticism and refinement. Its value, however great, will ultimately become "merely historical" in that it will no longer count as a useful component of the *current* stage in the discussion of the issues.

Every state-of-the-art configuration of a philosophical doctrine is inherently unstable.

Moreover, new conflicts constantly recur intrasystemically. New apories arise as we develop systems further and make divergent resolutions. Inconsistency breaks out again and again as we refine our answers for the nth level of approximation to the $(n + 1)$st. There is bound to be an ongoing succession of "family quarrels" within the various schools of thought.

Throughout the process envisaged by the aporetic model of philosophical development, the old diversities persist. The different programs created by different resolutions to *old* questions remain in place. All philosophers work within one or another long-established tradition; they cannot sever the links that bind them to the past of the subject. Old conflicts regarding fundamentals never die—they just take on a new and more sophisticated garb. The old alternatives remain intact in essentials, defined by the fundamental aporetic theses that later developments refine. The lines of resolution initially embarked upon need never hit a dead end—they can simply continue on their separate paths.

The Burden of History

Hegel saw the history of philosophy as a succession of systems, each system naturally giving rise to the next and each characteristic of the historical era in which it was developed—the whole process inexorably leading toward Hegel's own philosophy. But the idea that every age has its characteristic philosophy is profoundly wrong. Not only are alternatives always open, but at some level *of* approximation the same old alternatives continue to be open.[8] Unlike creative activity in music or the fine arts, philosophizing is not a matter of transiently all-embracing styles but of ever-recurrent doctrines. Dilthey was right in stressing, against Hegel, that the development *of* philosophy is not a sequential succession of all-dominant systems but an ongoing parallelism of conflicting systems that assume different historically conditioned configurations.[9] Our interest in the history of philosophy should never be merely historical, for it is by understanding the twists and turns by which our position has attained its present configuration in the forging of flavors of ongoing controversy that we can best understand exactly what that position amounts to.

Overall, what we have in philosophy is not the evolution of consensus but continuing controversy. The quarrel between idealists and realists, determinists and free-willers, skeptics and cognitivists, deontologists and consequentialists, and so on, all represent branchings in a river that flows on and on.

Dilthey was among the first to stress this and to make the enduring strife of systems a central plank of his theoretical platform:

> The contest among rival world-views cannot be brought to a decision at any significant point. The course of history effects a selection among them, but their main types stand forth alongside each other self-sufficiently, impassable yet indestructible. Owing their existence to no decisive demonstration, they can be destroyed by none. The individual styles and the particular formula tions of each type come to be "refuted," but their rooting in human life persists and fortifies and continually produces new forms.[10]

Philosophical history since classical antiquity unfolds as an ongoing refinement of preexisting doctrines, a development in whose course ever-more sophisticatedly divergent doctrines emerge from the fundamental discords of old, established programs. It is marked by the persistence of the conflict between the schools, an ongoing rivalry of systems.

The question "Is the natural world the product of the creative agency of an underlying intelligence?" has been debated by philosophers since antiquity. One tradition (stretching from Anaximander to Democritus to Hobbes and beyond) responds negatively. A second tradition (from Anaxagoras to Plato to Berkeley and beyond) takes an affirmative line. A third tradition (from Pyrrho to Kant to Carnap) wants to dismiss the question as inappropriate. There is no good reason to think that a metaphysical issue like this will ever be settled; the only reasonable stance is to expect an ongoing rivalry between these three competing schools of thought.

❦

In the end, philosophical development is a matter of ongoing conceptual innovation. And this has important consequences. For while we can roughly predict in advance what the underlying issues on the agenda of future philosophy will be—they will be, in essentials, those that have always been there: the problems of man's knowledge of the world and his place within it—we cannot foresee details of what solutions to these problems will be offered and what sorts of standards will be deployed to judge their adequacy. Questions of knowledge, justice, and duty will not go away—in some form or other they will always be there (though there will always be some Pyrrhonists who would have us jettison the lot). But by what conceptual contrivances these views will be argued is something regarding which we must, in the very nature of things, remain profoundly ignorant. Philosophizing is a creative process, and in philosophy, as in natural science, there is and can be no substance-oriented "law of inner development" with regard to matters of substantive detail. But what we certainly do have is an external, structurally oriented process of development that carries the discussion ever deeper into regions of increasing difficulty, elaboration, sophistication, and, all in all, complexity. And in the end we are liable to get in beyond our depth, ever unable to resolve matters at once completely and definitively. As regards ignorance we are never wholly out of the woods.

But don't philosophical issues fade away and die off? "Nobody could now win credence who asserted that to be is to be a quantity of water, however plausible that doctrine might have looked to Thales."[11] But matters are never that simple. The notion that everything in the world is composed of one uniform type of stuff that is highly changeable and "fluid"—that to be is to be a form of substance of which water is a useful paradigm—can certainly not be written off. Admittedly, philosophers are no longer preoccupied with the mental processes of angels! True enough! Yet philosophers have not ceased to contemplate the nature of superhuman intelligence—though they are nowadays more likely to discuss them in the setting of computers or extraterrestrial aliens than in that of angels. The point is that philosophical issues do not die out in essentials—they simply alter their form to accommodate themselves to new circum stances. We cannot issue death certificates in philosophy. Yes, problems do sometimes just fade away. But in general this happens only with more or less technical problems of nth order of detail. The basic problems al ways remain in place, firmly rooted in some fundamental element of the human condition.[12]

The Structure of Philosophical History

It is clear that on this basis why the study of the history of philosophy is an integral part of the study of the subject itself. One can only understand the character of current positions—can only grasp their need for all those distinctions—by retracing the steps that have brought matters to their present pass. Philosophical genealogy is crucial to comprehending the bearing of a philosophical concept, thesis, or argument. Only by following through the dialectical "family tree" of distinctions can we come to see the root issues out of which a philosophical doctrine arose and from which it draws its relevance to human concerns—and thus its significance.

The dialectical format for schematizing the developmental process in philosophy also opens up interesting prospects for analysis. For example, it makes it possible to raise certain historical questions that would otherwise seem wild and senseless. In considering how an antinomy defines a spectrum of competing positions, one can now pose the essentially negative question of why a certain theoretically available position was not actually taken—why a certain "ecological niche" in philosophy was allowed to stand empty at a certain juncture. One can ask in a perfectly meaningful way why certain philosophical positions were *not* taken at a particular stage in the development of the subject— and expect to receive an informative and illuminating response, perhaps in terms of the intellectual presuppositions or preconceptions of the day.

The dialectical model of philosophical development carries significant implications for philosophical historiography. For it indicates the desirability and explanatory utility of describing at least the major outlines of the course of philosophical history in terms of such an explicitly dialectical format. In highlighting points of similarity and difference, such a process serves to clarify the philosophical concepts and distinctions and theses at issue in the articulation of various philosophical positions. (The ancient Greek doxographers provide a pioneering if somewhat crude model in this respect.) An account in these terms is a most useful way to recast our perceptions of philosophical history.

We return once more to the promise that has been made again and again of a sketch of the history of philosophy (or some of its departments) on dialectical principles. Such an account would present, at least in outline, the succession of aporetic difficulties and apory-removing distinctions through which various philosophical schools of thought have evolved in interactive rivalry. As yet we have little more than illustrations of this programmatic prospect. But even this is enough to suggest that a fuller realization of the program would provide a most illuminating and valuable resource, affording a clearer and more cogent idea of the development of philosophy as an orderly process with a coherent developmental structure that endows it with a fundamental historical unity and integrity. It would enable us to supplement the purely biographical and chronological approach with a systematic account of the development of lines of thought rather than a disjointed-seeming series of ever-changing views of particular thinkers.

In our dealings with aporetic clusters and antinomies in philosophy, consistency, once reestablished, will not remain forever. For in resolving our problems we begin with the simplest viable solutions. But trouble invariably lurks around as yet unturned corners. The fact-coordinated character of philosophical concepts precludes the prospect of a global (universal, all-purpose) context in which their inner tensions can be resolved once and for all. As we elaborate our philosophical positions by following the standard and natural, indeed *inevitable*, policy of giving the most straightforward and "plausible" answers to different questions in different contexts, we find ourselves plunged into inconsistency; solutions adequate in one context are inadequate in another. And in consequence the history of philosophy consists largely in an ongoing confrontation between competing positions standing perpetually in conflict, though changing in detail through increasing sophistication and complexification.

Chapter 7

Ignorance and
Cognitive Horizons

Ignorance

The scope and limits of our knowledge is an issue that has been on the agenda of human concern since classical antiquity. And it is clearly an issue in which we have a significant stake. To be sure, we are not concerned here with personal ignorance—the contingent matter of the shortfall of a particular individual's knowledge. Rather, our interest is in what cannot be known.

There are, clearly, more facts (say, about things—be they abstract numbers or concrete realities) than one can ever come to know. So there are some facts that I will never learn. But of course my ignorance of many of these facts is shallow and contingent, relating to things that I could learn—that is, would come to know if I took the appropriate steps. But are there also facts that one could not possibly come to know, facts that are beyond one's cognitive reach?

In inquiring into this problem area, we are not interested in questions whose unanswerability resides merely in the contingent fact that certain information is not in practice accessible. "Did Julius Caesar hear a dog bark on his thirtieth birthday?" There is no possible way in which we can secure the needed information here and now. (Time travel is still impracticable.) Such questions are not inherently unanswerable, and it is unanswerability as a matter of principle that will concern us here.[1]

There are two principal sorts of unanswerable questions: those that are *locally* irresolvable, and those that are so *globally*. Locally unanswerable questions are those which a particular individual or group is unable to answer. An instance of such a question is: "What is an example of a fact of which you are altogether ignorant?" Clearly you cannot possibly manage to answer this, because whatever instance you adduce as such a fact must be something you know or believe to be such (that is, a fact), so that you cannot possibly be altogether ignorant of it. Yet on the other hand, it is clear that *somebody else* could readily be in the position to answer the question. Again, consider such questions as:

- What is an example of a problem that will never be considered by any human being?
- What is an example of an idea that will never occur to any human being?

There are sound reasons of general principle (the potential infinitude of problems and ideas; the inherent finitude of human intelligence) to hold that the items at issue in these questions (problems that will never be considered; ideas that will never occur) do actually exist. And it seems altogether plausible to think that other (nonhuman) hypothetically envisionable intelligences could well answer these questions correctly. But it is equally clear that we humans could never provide the requisite answers.

And looking beyond this, we can also contemplate the prospect of globally intractable questions such that nobody (among finite intelligences, at least) can possibly be in a position to answer them (in the strict sense described at the outset).

An example of such globally unanswerable questions can be provided by nontrivial but yet inherently uninstantiable predicates along the lines of

- What question is there that has never occurred to anybody?
- What occurrence is there that no one ever mentions?

There undoubtedly are such items, but of course they cannot be instantiated, so that questions which ask for examples here are inherently unanswerable.[2] With such answer-possessing but unanswerable questions it accordingly must transpire that the answer that, abstractly speaking, has to be there is one that cannot possibly be specified by way of particularized identification.

Intractable Questions about the Cognitive Future and Surd Generalities

But what does all this mean for knowledge? As already observed, the specification of unknowable facts is totally infeasible, since establishing factuality would automatically clash with unknowability. Knowledge being knowledge *of fact*, whatever instances of unknown truth that we can consider have to remain in the realm of conjecture rather than in that of knowledge. Given that *knowledge* fails us here, the most and best we can do is to resort to guesswork. Accordingly, let us now explore the prospect of making an at least plausible conjecture at specifying an unknowable fact.

Some questions are unanswerable for essentially practical reasons: We lack any prospect of securing effective means for their resolution. For reasons of contingent fact—the impracticability of time travel, say, or of space travel across vast distances. But such contingently grounded ignorance is not as bad as it gets. For some questions are in principle irresolvable in that purely theoretical reasons (rather than mere pivotal limitations) preclude the possibility of securing the information required for their resolution. Nevertheless, there is—or may be—no sound reason for dismissing such questions as meaningless, because a hypothetical being can be imagined by whom such a question can in theory be resolved. But given the inevitabilities of *our* relation as time-bound and finite intelligences, the question may be such that any prospect of resolution is precluded on grounds of general principle.

Are there any such meaningful yet intractable questions?

Our best strategy here is to consider the situation of natural science, focusing specifically on the problem of our knowledge of the scientific future. Clearly, to identify an insoluble scientific problem, we would have to show that a certain inherently appropriate scientific question is nevertheless such that its resolution lies beyond every (possible or imaginable) state of future science. This is obviously a *very* tall order—particularly so in view of our inevitably deficient grasp of future science. After all, we cannot foresee what we cannot conceive. Our questions—let alone answers—cannot outreach the limited horizons of our concepts. Having never contemplated electronic computing machines as such, the ancient Romans could also venture no predictions about their impact on the social and economic life of the twenty-first century. Clever though he unquestionably was, Aristotle could not have pondered the issues of quantum electrodynamics. The scientific questions of the future are—at least in part—bound to be conceptually inaccessible to the inquirers of the present. The question of just how the cognitive agenda of some future date will be constituted is clearly irresolvable for us now. Not only can we not anticipate future discoveries now, we cannot even prediscern the questions that will arise as time moves on and cognitive progress with it.[3]

Scientific inquiry is a venture in innovation. And in consequence, it lies in the nature of things that present science can never speak decisively for future science, and present science cannot predict the specific discoveries of future inquiry. After all, our knowledge of the present cannot encompass that of the future—if we could know about those future discoveries now they would not have to await the future. Accordingly, knowledge about what science will achieve over all—and thus just where it will be going in the long run—is beyond the reach of attainable knowledge at this or any other particular stage of the scientific "state of the art."

Omar Khayyam lamented our human ignorance of what is to follow for us after this earthly life: "Into this Universe, and *Why* not knowing, . . . I know not *Whither*, willy-nilly blowing." But in this regard the human situation vis-à-vis the condition of the merely worldly future is not all that different from that of the afterlife. In particular, it is in principle infeasible for us to tell now but only how future science will answer present questions, but even what questions will figure on the question agenda of the future—let alone what answers they will engender. In this regard, as in others, it lies in the inevitable realities of our condition that the detailed nature of our ignorance is—for us at least—hidden away in an impenetrable fog.

It is clear on this basis that the question "Are there non-decidable scientific questions that scientific inquiry will never resolve, even were it to continue *ad indefinitum*?"—the insolubilia question, as we may call it—is one that cannot possibly ever be settled in a decisive way. After all, how could we possibly establish that a question Q about some issue of fact will continue to be *posable but unanswerable* in every future state of science, seeing that we cannot now circumscribe the changes that science might undergo in the future? And, since this is so, our question itself is self-instantiating: it is a question regarding an aspect of reality (of which, of course, science itself is a part) that scientific inquiry will never—at any specific state of the art—be in a position to settle decisively.[4]

The long and short of it is that the very impredictability of future knowledge renders the identification of insolubilia impracticable. (In this regard, it is effectively a bit of good fortune that we are ignorant about the lineaments of our ignorance.)[5] We are cognitively myopic with respect to future knowledge. And for this reason there are questions such as that instanced above that are inherently irresolvable—thought of course, educated guesswork is something else again.

Given that our explicit knowledge of facts is always mediated through language, it will be confined to truths. But just exactly what does all this mean for the reach of knowledge? What are we to make of the numerical disparity between facts and truths, between what is knowable in itself and what we language-bound intelligences can actually manage to know? It means, of course, that our knowledge is going to be incomplete. Just what does this portend?

Even though the actual thought and knowledge of finite beings is destined to be ever finite, it nevertheless has no fixed and determinate limits. Let us return to an already cited analogy. No matter how far out we go in counting integers, we never get beyond the range of the finite. Even so with facts. There is a limit beyond which we *will* never get. But there is no limit beyond which we *can* never get. For the circumstance that there is always room for linguistic variation—for new symbols, new combinations, new ideas, new truths, and new knowledge—creates a potential for pushing our thought ever further.

Moreover, any adequate account of inquiry must recognize that the process of information acquisition at issue in science is a process of *conceptual* innovation. Caesar did not know—and in the then-extant state of the cognitive art could not have known—that his sword contained tungsten and carbon. There will always be facts about a thing that we do not *know* because we cannot even *express* them in the prevailing conceptual order of things. To grasp such a fact means taking a perspective of consideration that as yet we simply do not have, since the state of knowledge (or purported knowledge) has not reached a point at which such a consideration is *feasible*. The ongoing progress of scientific inquiry always leaves various facts about the things of this world wholly outside the cognitive range of the inquirers of any particular period. Even though the thought of finite beings is destined ever to be finite, it nevertheless has no fixed and determinable limits.

The line of thought operative in these deliberations was already mooted by Kant:

> [I]n natural philosophy, human reason admits of *limits* ["excluding limits," *Schranken*] but not of *boundaries* ["terminating limits," *Grenzen*], namely, it admits that something

indeed lies without it, at which it can never arrive, but not that it will at any point find completion in its internal progress. . . . [T]he possibility of new discoveries is infinite: and the same is the case with the discovery of new properties of nature, of new powers and laws by continued experience and its rational combination. . . .[6]

And here Kant was right—even on the Leibnizian principles considered at the outset of this discussion. The cognitive range of finite beings is indeed limited. But it is also boundless because it is not limited in a way that blocks the prospect of cognitive access to ever new and continually different facts, thereby affording an ever ampler and ever more adequate account of reality.[7]

Skepticism calls into question the very possibility of knowledge. And this doesn't make much sense.[8] But a theory of cognitive finitude—of limits to knowledge—is something else again. Such a thing makes very good sense indeed. For the reality of the situation of finite knowers is that there are limits to knowledge. The determination—let alone explanation—of universal but contingent fact is something beyond the cognitive reach of finite beings. In the pursuit of knowledge, and especially of knowledge that runs as wide and deep as that to which philosophy aspires, we meet ever-increasing obstacles. And this makes for an eventual unavoidability of issues whose resolution calls for resources beyond the limited means at our disposal. Its efforts to domesticate cognitively a world of virtually endless complexity, variety, and detail ultimately impels philosophy into a realm of intractible questions and insolubilia. The reality of it is that in philosophy as in life we simply cannot manage to have it all our own way. We have to come to terms with limits and limitations.

Insolubilia Then and Now

A medieval insolubilium was represented by a question that cannot be answered satisfactorily one way or another because every possible answer is unavailable on grounds of *a logical insufficiency of inherent coherence.* Such an insolubilium poses a paradox. By contrast, a modern insolubilium poses a puzzle. It is represented by a question that cannot be answered satisfactorily one way or another because every possible answer is unavailable on grounds of *an evidential insufficiency of accessible information.*

An example of the former (medieval) sort of logical *insolubilium* is posed by the self-referential statement: "This sentence is false." Is this statement true or not? Whatever answer we give, be it yes or no, we are in deep trouble.

But what about factual *insolubilia* of the modern type—informatively unanswerable questions?

Consider some possible examples of this phenomenon. In 1880 the German physiologist, philosopher, and historian of science Emil du Bois-Reymond published a widely discussed lecture entitled *The Seven Riddles of the Universe* (*Die sieben Welträtsel*), in which he maintained that some of the most fundamental problems regarding the workings of the world were irresolvable. Du Bois-Reymond was a rigorous mechanist. On his view, nonmechanical modes of inquiry cannot produce adequate results, and the limit of our secure knowledge of the world is confined to the range where purely mechanical principles can be applied. As for all else, we not only *do not* have but *cannot* in principle obtain reliable knowledge. Under the banner of the slogan *ignoramus et ignorabimus* ("we *do not* know and *shall never* know"), Du Bois-Reymond maintained a skeptically agnostic position with respect to basic issues in physics (the nature of matter and of force, and the ultimate source of motion) and psychology (the origin of sensation and of consciousness). These issues are simply *insolubilia* that transcend man's scientific capabilities. Certain fundamental biological problems he regarded as unsolved, but perhaps in principle soluble (though very difficult): the origin of life, the adaptiveness of organisms, and the development of language and reason. And as regards the seventh riddle—the problem of freedom of the will—he was undecided.

The position of Du Bois-Reymond was swiftly and sharply contested by the zoologist Ernest Haeckel in his book *Die Welträtsel*, published in 1889, which soon attained a great popularity. Far from being intractable or even insoluble—so Haeckel maintained—the riddles of Du Bois-Reymond had all virtually been solved. Dismissing the problem of free will as a pseudoproblem—since free will "is a pure dogma [that] rests on mere illusion and in reality does not exist at all"— Haeckel turned with relish to the remaining riddles. Problems of the origin of life, of sensation, and of consciousness Haeckel regarded as solved—or solvable—by appeal to the theory of evolution. Questions of the nature of matter and force he regarded as solved by modern physics except for one residue: the problem (perhaps less scientific than metaphysical) of the ultimate origin of matter and its laws. This "problem of substance" was the only remaining riddle recognized by Haeckel, and it was not really a problem of science: in discovering the "fundamental law of the conservation of matter and force" science had done pretty much what it could do with respect to this problem—the rest that remained was metaphysics, with which the scientist had no proper concern. Haeckel summarized his position as follows:

> The number of world-riddles has been continually diminishing in the course of the nineteenth century through the aforesaid progress of a true knowledge of nature. Only one comprehensive riddle of the universe now remains—he problem of substance. . . . [But now] we have the great, comprehensive "law of substance," the fundamental law of the constancy of matter and force. The fact that substance is everywhere subject to eternal movement and transformation gives it the character also of the universal law of evolution. As this supreme law has been firmly established, and all others are subordinate to it, we arrive at a conviction of the universal unity of nature and the eternal validity of its laws. From the gloomy *problem* of substance we have evolved the clear *law* of substance.[9]

The basic structure of Haeckel's teaching is clear: science is rapidly nearing a state where all the big problems have been solved. What remains unresolved is not so much a *scientific* as a *metaphysical* problem. In science itself, the big battle is virtually at an end, and the work that remains to be done is pretty much a matter of mopping-up operations.

But is this rather optimistic position tenable? Can we really dismiss the prospect of authentic insolubilia? Let us explore this issue more closely.

Cognitive Limits

To begin with, there is the prospect of what might be called the *weak limitation* inherent in the circumstance that there are certain issues on its agenda that science cannot resolve *now*. However, this condition of weak limitation is perfectly compatible with the circumstance that *every* question raisable at this stage will *eventually* be answered at a future juncture. A contrasting prospect in which the question-resolving capacity of our knowledge may be limited might be called *strong limitation*:

> *Strong Limitation (The Existence of Insolubilia).* There will (at some juncture) be then-posable questions that will *never* obtain answers, meaningful questions whose resolution lies beyond the reach of science altogether—questions that will remain ever unsolved on the cognitive agenda.

Such strong limitation poses the existence of immortal questions— permanently unanswerable questions (general insolubilia) that admit of no resolution within any cognitive corpus we are able to bring to realization.

However, for there to be insolubilia it is certainly not necessary that anything be said about the current *availability* of the insoluble question. The prospect of its actual identification *at this or indeed any other particular prespecified historical juncture is wholly untouched.* Even a position that holds that there indeed *are* insolubilia certainly need not regard them as being identifiable at the present state of the art of scientific development. One can accordingly also move beyond the two preceding theses to the yet stronger principle of

> *Hyperlimitation (The existence of* identifiable *insolubilia).* Our present-day cognitive agenda includes certain here-and-now specifiable and scientifically meaningful questions whose resolution lies beyond the reach of science altogether.

Awkwardly, however, a claim to identify insolubilia by pinpointing here-and-now issues that future inquiry will never resolve can readily go awry. Charles S. Peirce has put the key point trenchantly:

> For my part, I cannot admit the proposition of Kant—that there are certain impassable bounds to human knowledge. . . . The history of science affords illustrations enough of the folly of saying that this, that, or the other can never be found out. Auguste Comte said that it was clearly impossible for man ever to learn anything of the chemical constitution of the fixed stars, but before his book had reached its readers the discovery which he had announced as impossible had been made. Legendre said of a certain proposition in the theory of numbers that, while it appeared to be true, it was most likely beyond the powers of the human mind to prove it; yet the next writer on the subject gave six independent demonstrations of the theorem.[10]

To identify an insoluble problem, we would have to show that a certain inherently appropriate question is such that its resolution lies beyond every (possible or imaginable) state of future science. This task is clearly a rather tall order. Its realization is clearly difficult, but not in principle impossible.

Observe, to begin with, that even if we agree with Peirce that science is en route to a completion, we may well always—at any given time—remain at a remove from ultimacy. For as long as the body of knowledge continues to grow, there will still remain scope for the possibility of insolubilia. Even a science asymptotically approaching completion can accommodate a fixed region of unresolvability, as long as the scope of that science itself is growing. That is, even if the *fraction* of unresolved questions converges asymptotically to zero, the *number* of unresolved questions may be ever growing in the context of an expanding science. For consider the following:

No. of questions on the agenda	100	1000	10,000	10k
Fraction of unresolved questions	$\frac{1}{2}$	$\frac{1}{4}$	$\frac{1}{8}$	$(\frac{1}{2})^{k-1}$
No. of unresolved questions	50	250	1,250	$10^k \times (\frac{1}{2})^{k-1}$

These figures indicate that there is room for insolubilia even within the setting of an approach to asymptotic completeness. And this points toward a prospect that merits closer scrutiny.

Identifying Insolubilia

To elucidate the prospect of identifying insolubilia, let us resume the theme of the progressive nature of knowledge, and continue the earlier considerations of second-order questions about future knowledge. Specifically, let us focus even more closely upon the historicity of knowledge development.

The limits of one's information set unavoidable limits to one's predictive capacities. In particular, we cannot foresee what we cannot conceive. Our questions—let alone answers—cannot outreach the limited horizons of our concepts. Having never contemplated electronic computing machines as such, the ancient Romans could also venture no predictions about their impact on the social and economic life of the twenty-first century. Clever though he unquestionably was, Aristotle could not have pondered the issues of quantum electrodynamics. The scientific questions of the future are—at least in part—bound to be conceptually inaccessible to the inquirers of the present. The question of just how the cognitive agenda of some future date will be constituted is clearly irresolvable for us now. Not only can we not anticipate future discoveries now, we cannot even prediscern the questions that will arise as time moves on and cognitive progress with it. We are cognitively myopic with respect to future knowledge. It is in principle infeasible for us to say now what questions will figure in the erotetic agenda of the future, let alone what answers they will engender.

But, of course, all of these are, by hypothesis, issues that will resolve themselves in the fullness of time. We have not as yet identified an insolubilium that can never be satisfactorily resolved.

To address this question, consider, however, the thesis:

> (T)   It will always be the case that there will come a time when all of the ever-resolved questions then on our question-agenda will be resolved within one hundred years.

And now let Q^* be the question: "Is T true or not?" It is clear that to answer this question Q^* one way or the other we would need to have cognitive mastery over the question agenda of all future times. And, as emphasized above, just this is something that we cannot manage to achieve. By their very nature as such, the discoveries of the future are unavailable at present. Thus, Q^* illustrates the sort of case we are looking for: It affords an example of a specific and perfectly meaningful question that we are in effect always and ever unable to resolve convincingly—irrespective of what the date on the calendar happens to read.

Of course, someone may possibly be minded to complain as follows:

> You are not giving me what I want. For let us distinguish between a base-level question in which no (essential) inference to questions and question agendas is made and a metalevel question in which there is an uneliminable reference to questions and question agendas. What I want is an example—a definitively specified instance—of an insolubilium at the base level of substantive questions about the real world.

To such a complainer one can respond as follows:

> In its own way, your complaint is well taken; and indeed it seems to be pretty much in the spirit of

> Peirce's telling observation just quoted above. But it is worthwhile to look in a somewhat different light at this very question that you have just raised, viz., "Are there any base-level factual insolubilia." The reality of it is that it is difficult or impossible to imagine that this is an issue that could be settled convincingly one way or the other in any state of actually available information. And so this question itself is a pretty good candidate for an insolubilium—though, to be sure, not at the base level.

Clearly the complaint under consideration cannot accomplish its intended mission.

Relating Knowledge to Ignorance

In any event, however, while there indeed are scientific insolubilia—and we can actually identify some of them—the fact remains that detailed knowledge about the *extent* of our ignorance is unavailable to us. For what is at stake with this issue of extent is the ratio of the manifold of what one does know to the manifold of what one does not. And it is impossible in the nature of things for me to get a clear fix on the latter. For the actual situation is not that of a crossword puzzle or of a geographic exploration where the size of the terra incognita can be somehow measured in advance of securing the details that are going to be filled in. We can form no sensible estimate of the imponderable domain of what can be known but is not. To be sure, we can manage to compare what one person or group knows with what some other person or group knows. But mapping the realm of what is knowable as such is something that inevitably is beyond our powers. And for this reason any questions about the cognitive completeness of our present knowledge are and will remain inexorably unresolvable.

There are, of course, finite fields of knowledge. There is only so much you can know (nonrelationally, at least) about the content of Boston's 1995 telephone directory, namely, the totality of what is in its pages. That is only the case because here "what *can be* known" and "what is known" actually coincide. But this sort of thing is the case only in very special circumstances and never with respect to areas of natural science such as medicine or physics that deal with the products of nature at a level of generality.

Yet although ignorance lies at the core of the present discussion, it is not an exercise in radical skepticism. It does not propose to take the pessimistic line of a cognitive negativism to the effect that knowledge about the world is unavailable to us. Instead, what is being contemplated here is (1) that despite whatever we may come to know there are some matters on which we are destined to remain ignorant, and (2) that among the things that we can get to know about are various facts about the nature and extent of our own ignorance.

That our knowledge is sufficient for our immediate purposes—specifically, by enabling us to answer the questions we then and there have before us—is something that is in principle readily determinable. But that it is *theoretically* adequate to answer not just our present questions but those that will grow out of them in the future is something we can never manage to establish. For it is clear that the sensible management of ignorance is something that requires us to operate in the realm of practical considerations exactly because the knowledge required for theoretical adequacy on this subject is—by hypothesis—not at our disposal. We have no cogently rational alternative to proceed, here as elsewhere, subject to the basic pragmatic principle of having to accept the best that we can do as good enough.

And so we return to the point made at the very outset: the ironic, though in some ways fortunate, fact is that one of the things about which we are most decidedly ignorant is the detailed nature of our ignorance itself. We simply cannot make a reliable assessment of the extent of our ignorance.

Notes

Chapter 1. Philosophical Principles

This chapter is a revised version of an essay of the same title in the *Review of Metaphysics* 59 (2005).

1. Plato, *Phaedrus* 101E and 107B.
2. Aristotle, *Metaphysics* 4.1.1012b34ff.
3. Aquinas, *Summa Theologica* 1.33, 1.
4. Recall that to be a "man of principles" is to honor the rules, to "play it by the book" and not to see oneself entitled to count as an exception—entitled to have things one's own way irrespective of the rules that hold for others.
5. Logic is something of an exception, since it is (traditionally seen as) a part of philosophy as well as a guide to its conduct. Because the principles of logic represent requisites of cogent communication, they hold ubiquitously in all domains—and accordingly govern sensible philosophical discourse as well.
6. On this issue, see Nicholas Rescher, *The Strife of Systems* (Pittsburgh: University of Pittsburgh Press, 1995).
7. Bertrand Russell, "On Denoting," *Mind* 14 (1905); pp 479–93. On the larger issues, see Nicholas Rescher *Essays in Philosophical Analysis* (Pittsburgh: University of Pittsburgh Press, 1969), pp. 73–109.
8. On Theophrastus's dictum and its role in the theory of modal syllogisms, see I. M. BocheÒski, *La logique Theophraste*, Publications de l'Université de Fribourg en Suisse, n.s., no. 31 (Fribourg en Suisse;Université de Fribourg en Suisse: 1947. On Aristotle's position, see N. Rescher, "Aristotle's Theory of Modal Syllogisms and its Interpretation," *The Critical Approach to Science and Philosophy*, ed. M. Bunge (London: Free Press, 1964), pp. 152–77.
9. Arthur Conan Doyle, "The Sign of Four" (1890).
10. Aristotle, *De incessu animalium* 1.3.8; *Politica* 1.2; *De caelo* 1.4.
11. William of Ockham, *Opera Philosophica*, vol. 1 (St. Bonaventure, N.Y.: Editiones Instituti Franciscani Universitatis S. Bonaventurae, 1974), pp. 185 et passim. See also Jen P. Beckmann, *Wilhelm von* (Munich: C. H. Beck, 1995), pp. 42–47.
12. See Beckmann, *Ockham*, pp. 42–47.

Chapter 2. Aporetic Method in Philosophy

This chapter originally appeared in *Review of Metaphysics* 41 (1987): 283–97.

1. The word derives from the Greek ἀπορία on analogy with "harmony" or "melody" or, indeed, "analogy" itself.

2. The conception of plausibility (and in particular its difference from the more familiar conception of *probability)* is explained in Nicholas Rescher, *Plausible Reasoning* (Assen: Van Gorcum, 1976).

3. To be sure, philosophers positioned in different experiential contexts will accomplish this differently, because their judgments of priority are bound to differ.

4. The aporetic nature of philosophy and its implications are explored in detail in Rescher, *Strife of Systems.* The book is also available in Spanish, Italian, and German translations.

Chapter 3. On Distinctions in Philosophy

1. See Alexander Bain, *Mental Science* (1868; rpt., New York: Arno Press, 1973) 2:82f.; and compare William James, *The Principles of Psychology* (New York: H. Holt and Company, 1890), pp. 242ff.

2. These considerations were elaborated in detail by Duns Scotus, especially in his *Opus Oxoniensis.*

3. See, for example, René Descartes, *Principia philosophiae* 1.60ff.

4. Frank P. Ramsey, *The Foundations of Mathematics and Other Logical Essays*, ed. R. B. Braithwaite (London: Kegan Paul, Trench, and Trübner, 1931), pp. 115–16.

5. This general position that philosoophical problems involve antinomic situations from which there are only finity many exits (which, in general, the historical course of philosophical development actually indicates) is foreshadowed inthe deliberations of Wilhelm Dilthey. See his *Gesammelte Schriften*, vol. 8 (Stuttgart: Teubner; Göttingen: Vandenhoeck and Ruprecht, 1961), p. 138.

Chapter 4. Respect Neglect and Misassimilation as Fallacies of Philosophical Distinctions

This chapter is a slightly revised version of my *Philosophy and Phenomenological Research* 65 (2005).

1. See Michael Krausz, ed., *Is There a Single Right Interpretation* (University Park PA: Pennsylvania State University Press, 2002).

2. Aristotle, *Metaphysics* 3.2996b.28ff.; idem, *On Interpretation* 6.17a.33ff. On the issues see R. M. Dancy, *Sense and Contradiction: A Study in Aristetle* (Dordrecht: D. Reidel, 1975).

Chapter 5. Systemic Interconnectedness and Explanatory Holism in Philosophy

1. David Hume, *Dialogues Concerning Natural Religion*, pt. 2.

2. David Hume, *A Treatise of Human Nature*, bk. 1, pt 3, sec. 3; or idem, *Dialogues*, pt. 9.

3. Paul Edwards, in *The Cosmological Argument*, ed. Donald R. Burrill (New York: Doubleday, 1967), pp. 113–14.

4. G. W. Leibniz, "On the Radical Organization of Things" (1697), in *G. W. Leibniz: Collected Papers,* ed. L. E. Loemker (Dordrecht: D. Reidel, 1959), pp. 486–87.

5. Relevant aspects of the fallacy of composition are discussed in William L. Rowe, "The Fallacy of Composition," *Mind* 71 (1964). See also C. C. Hamblin, *Fallacies* (London: Methuen, 1970).

6. Luwig Wittgenstein, *Notebooks* (Oxford: Blackwell, 1961), pp. 45, 50, 64.

7. Ibid, p. 47.

8. Ibid., p. 46.

9. Ludwig Wittgenstein, "Some Remarks on Logical Form," *Proceedings of the Aristotelian Society*, supp. vol. 9 (1929): 162–71.

10. Bertrand Russell, "The Philosophy of Logical Atomism," Monist, vol. 12 (1918); reprinted in J. O. Urmson, *Philosophical Analysis* (Oxford: Clarendon Press, 1956).

11. See Kuno Lorenz, *Arithmetik und Logik als Spiele* (Kiel: Kiel University, 1961); and W. Stegmüller, "Logical Systems Relative to the Validating Concepts of P. Lorenzen and K. Lorenz," *Notre Dame Journal of Formal Logic* 5 (1964): 81–112.

12. For a concise exposition of logical atomism, see John Passmore, *A Hundred Years of Philosophy* (Harmondsworth, UK: Penguin Books, 1968); or Avrum Stroll, *Twentieth Century Analytic Philosophy* (New York: Columbia University Press, 2000).

13. A. N. Whitehead, *Process and Reality: An Essay in Cosmooogy* (New York: Macmillan, 1929); Critical edition by D. R. Griffin and D. W. Sherbourne (New York: Macmillan, 1978). For further elaboration and references to the extensive literature, see Nicholas Rescher, *Process Metaphysics* (Albany: SUNY Press, 1961). Whitehead's work has found a substantial following whose members have construed their master's teachings in rather different ways.

14. Rudolf Carnap, *Der logische Aufbau der Welt* (Berlin-Schlactensee: Weltkreis-Verlag, 1928).

15. One these issues, see Annette Baier, "The Search for Basic Actions," *American Philosophical Quarterly* 8 (1971): 161–70. References to further literature can be found here.

16. One these issues, see ibid.

17. This discussion originated in a paper read at the annual meeting of the American Philosophical Society in Athens, Georgia, in March 2004.

18. See Bertrand Russell and F. C. Copleston, "The Existence of God: A Debate between Bertrand Russell and Father F. C. Copleston," in *The Existence of God*, ed. John Hick (New York: Macmillan, 1964).

19. Various relevant aspects of existence explanation are dealt within William L. Rowe, *The Cosmological Argument* (Princeton, N.J.: Princeton University Press, 1975).

20. Ronald W. Hepburn, "Cosmological Argument for the Existence of God," in *The Encyclopedia of Philosophy*, ed. Paul Edwards (New York: Macmillan, 1967), 2:235; italics supplied. See also Ronald W. Hepburn, *Christianity and Paradox* (London: Walls, 1958), pp. 167–68.

21. William James, "The Sentiment of Rationality," in *The Will to Believe and Other Essays in Popular Philosophy* (New York: Longmans, Green, 1897), p. 109.

22. Michael Dummett, "Truth," *Proceedings of the Aristotelian Society* 59 (1956–59): 159–70, reprinted in *Truth or Other Enigmas* (Cambridge, Mass: Harvard University Press, 1978). C. S. Pierce sometimes asserted a similar view.

23. The aspect of objectivity was justly stressed in the "Second Analogy" of Kant's *Critique of Pure Reason*, though this discussion rests on ideas already contemplated by Leibniz. See Immanuel Kant, *Philosophische Schriften*, ed. C. I. Gerhardt, vol. 7 (Berlin: Weidmannsche Buchhandlung, 1890), pp. 319–20.

24. Further aspects of the systemic nature of truth are explored in Nicholas Rescher, *The Coherence Theory of Truth* (Oxford: Clarendon Press, 1973).

25. John Kekes, *The Nature of Philosophy* (Totowa, N.J.: Rowman and Littlefield, 1980), p. 196.

Chapter 6. The Structure of Philosophical Dialectic

1. William James, *A Pluralistic Universe* (New York: Longmans, Green, 1909), p. 321.

2. On Aristotle's dialectic, see especially book 1 of the *Topics*. For interpretative expositions, see J. D. G. Evans, *Aristotle's Concept of Dialectics* (Cambridge: Cambridge University Press, 1977); and G. E. L. Owen, ed., *Aristotle on Dialectic* (Oxford: Clarendon Press, 1968).

3. The exact nature of Hegel's own dialectic is the subject of much interpretative disagreement, and the present account is rather as a matter of Hegelian inspiration than of legal interpretation. For a spectrum of diverse views, see Dieter Henrich ed., *Die Wissenschaft der Logik und die Logik der Reflection*, Hegel Studien, supplemental vol. 18 (Bonn: Bouvier Verlag, 1978).

4. "TIME Essay: What (If Anything) to Expect from Today's Philosophers," *Time*, January 7, 1966, p. 25.

5. Dilthey, *Gesammelte Schriften*, 8:134.

6. Immanuel Kant, *Prolegomena to Any Future Metaphysics*, trans. L. W. Beck (Indianapolis: Bobbs-Merrill, 1950), p. 3.

7. Dilthey, *Gesammelte Schriften*, 8:226.

8. To say this is not, of course, to deny that philosophers of a given era usually share a great many assumptions.

9. Dilthey, *Gesammelte Schriften*, 8:131, 8:134.

10. Ibid., 86–87.

11. John Passmore, *Philosophical Reasoning* (London: Duckworth, 1961), p. 39.

12. Some issues relevant to this chapter are treated in the author's *The Strife of Systems* (Pittsburgh: University of Pittsburgh Press, 1985).

Chapter 7. Ignorance and Cognitive Horizons

1. Nor will we be concerned here with the issue of indemonstrable truths and unanswerable questions in pure mathematics. Our concern is only with *factual* truths, and the issue of truth in such formal disciplines as mathematics or logic will be left aside.

2. This issue here is one of so-called vagrant predicates that have no known address.

3. Of course these questions already exist—what lies in the future is not their existence but their presence on the agenda of active concern.

4. And this issue cannot be settled by supposing a mad scientist who explodes the superbomb that blows the earth to smithereens and extinguishes all organic life as

we know it. For the prospect cannot be precluded that intelligent life will evolve elsewhere. And even if we contemplate the prospect of a "big crunch" that is a reverse "big bang" and implodes our universe into an end, the project can never be precluded that at the other end of the big crunch, so to speak, another era of cosmic development awaits.

5. That contingent future development is by nature cognitively intractable, even for God, was a prospect supported even by some of the scholastics. On this issue see Marilyn McCord Adams, *William Ockham*, vol. 2 (Notre Dame, Ind.: University of Notre Dame Press, 1987), chap. 27.

6. Kant, *Prolegomena to Any Future Metaphysics*, sec. 57. Compare the following passage from Charles Sanders Peirce: "For my part, I cannot admit the proposition of Kant—that there are certain impassable bounds to human knowledge. . . . The history of science affords illustrations enough of the folly of saying that this, that, or the other can never be found out. Auguste Comte said that it was clearly impossible for man ever to learn anything of the chemical constitution of the fixed stars, but before his book had reached its readers the discovery which he had announced as impossible had been made. Legendre said of a certain proposition in the theory of numbers that, while it appeared to be true, it was most likely beyond the powers of the human mind to prove it; yet the next writer on the subject gave six independent demonstrations of the theorem." C. S. Peirce, *Collected Papers*, 2nd ed. (Cambridge, Mass.: Harvard University Press, 1931–58), vol. 6, sec. 6.556.

7. This discussion has profited from the constructive comments of several Pittsburgh colleagues, including Jason Dickinson, Mickey Perloff, and Laura Ruetsche.

8. For my position on the issue, see Nicholas Rescher, *Scepticism* (Oxford: Blackwell, 1980).

9. Ernest Haeckel, *The Riddle of the Universe at the Close of the Nineteenth Century* (London: Watts, 1900), p. 183.

10. Peirce, *Collected Papers.*

Bibliography

Adams, Marilyn McCord. *William Ockham.* 2 vols. Notre Dame, Ind.: University of Notre Dame Press, 1987.

Austin, J. L. *Philosophical Papers.* Oxford: Clarendon Press, 1961.

Bain, Alexander. *Mental Science.* 1868. Reprint, New York: Arno Press, 1973.

Baier, Annette. "The Search for Basic Actions." *American Philosophical Quarterly* 8 (1971): 161–70.

Beckmann, Jan P. *Wilhelm von Ockham.* Munich: C. H. Beck. 1995.

Bocheński, I. M. *La logique de Theophraste.* Publications de l'Université de Fribourg en Suisse, n.s., no. 31. Fribourg en Suisse: Université de Fribourg en Suisse, 1947.

Carnap, Rudolf. *Der logische Aufbau der Welt.* Berlin-Schlachtensee: Weltkreis-Verlag, 1928.

Dancy, R. M. *Sense and Contradiction: A Study in Aristotle.* Dordrecht: D. Reidel, 1975.

Dilthey, Wilhelm. *Gesammelte Schriften.* Stuttgart: Teubner; Göttingen: Vandenhoeck and Ruprecht, 1961.

Doyle, Arthur Conan. "The Sign of Four." (1890).

Dummett, Michael. "Truth." *Proceedings of the Aristotelian Society* 59 (1956–59): 159–70. Reprinted in *Truth and Other Enigmas.* Cambridge, Mass.: Harvard University Press, 1978.

Edwards, Paul. In *The Cosmological Argument*, edited by Donald R. Burrill (New York: Doubleday, 1967), 113–14.

Haeckel, Ernest. *Die sieben Welträtsel.* Translated as *The Riddle of the Universe at the Close of the Nineteenth Century-.* London: Watts & Co., 1900.

Hamblin, C. C. *Fallacies.* London: Methuen, 1970.

Henrich, Dieter, ed. *Die Wissenschaft der Logik und die Logik der Reflection.* Hegel Studien, supplemental vol. 18. Bonn: Bouvier Verlag, 1978.

Hepburn, Ronald W. "Cosmological Argument for the Existence of God." In vol. 2 of *The Encyclopedia of Philosophy*, edited by Paul Edwards. New York: Macmillan, 1962.

Hick, John, ed. *The Existence of God.* New York: Macmillan, 1964.

James, William. *A Pluralistic Universe.* New York: Longmans, Green, 1909.

———. *Principles of Psychology.* New York: H. Holt and Company, 1890.

Kant, Immanuel. *Philosophische Schriften.* Edited by C. I. Gerhardt. Vol. 7. Berlin: Weidmannsche Buchhandlung, 1890.

———. *Prolegomena to Any Future Metaphysics.* Translated by Lewis W. Beck. Indianapolis: Bobbs-Merrill, 1950.

Kekes, John. *The Nature of Philosophy.* Totowa, N.J.: Rowman and Littlefield, 1980.

Krausz, M., ed. *Is There a Single Right Interpretation?* University Park: Pennsylvania State University Press, 2002.

Leibniz, G. W. *De l'horizon de la doctrine humaine.* Edited by Michel Fichant. Paris: Vrin, 1991.

———. "On the Radical Organization of Things." 1697. Reprinted in *G. W. Leibniz: Collected Papers*, edited by L. E. Loemker, pp. 486–87. Dordrecht: D. Reidel, 1959.

Lorenz, Kuno. *Arithmetick und Logik als Spiele.* Kiel: Kiel University, 1962.

Ockham, William of. *Opera Philosophica.* Vol. 1. St. Bonaventure, N.Y.: Editiones Instituti Franciscani Universitatis Bonaventurae, 1974.

Passmore, John. *A Hundred Years of Philosophy.* Harmondsworth, U.K.: Penguin Books, 1968.

———. *Philosophical Reasoning.* London: G. Duckworth, 1961.

Pears, D. F. "Logical Atomism." In *The Revolution of Philosophy.* New York: St. Martin's Press, 1956.

Peirce, Charles Sanders. *Collected Papers.* 2nd ed. Cambridge, Mass.: Harvard University Press, 1931–58.

Ramsey, F. P. *The Foundations of Mathematics and Other Logical Essays.* Edited by R. B. Braithwaite. London: Kegan Paul, Trench, Trübner, 1931.

Rescher, Nicholas. "Aporetic Method in Philosophy." *Review of Metaphysics* 1 (1987): 283–97.

———. "Aristotle's Theory of Modal Syllogisms and Its Interpretation." In *The Critical Approach to Science and Philosophy*, pp. 152–77. London: Free Press, 1964.

———. *Essays in Philosophical Analysis.* Pittsburgh: University of Pittsburgh Press, 1969.

———. *Hypothetical Reasoning.* Amsterdam: North Holland Publishing Company, 1964.

———. "Philosophical Principles." *Review of Metaphysics* 59 (2005).

———. *Philosophical Standardism.* Pittsburgh: University of Pittsburgh Press, 1994.

———. *Plausible Reasoning.* Assen: Van Gorcum, 1976.

————. *Process Metaphysics*. Albany: State University of New York Press, 1961.

————. *Scepticism*. Oxford: Blackwell, 1980.

————. *The Strife of Systems*. Pittsburgh: University of Pittsburgh Press, 1985.

Rowe, William L. *The Cosmological Argument*. Princeton, N.J.: Princeton University Press, 1975.

————. "The Fallacy of Composition." *Mind* 71 (1964).

Russell, Bertrand. "On Denoting." *Mind* 14 (1905): 479–93.

————. "The Philosophy of Logical Atomism." *Monist* 18 (1918).

Stegmüller, Wolfgang. "Logical Systems Relative to the Validating Concepts of P. Lorenzer and K. Lorenz *Notre Dame Journal of Formal Logic* 5 (1964): 81–112.

Stroll, Avrum. *Twentieth-Century Analytic Philosophy*. New York: Columbia University Press, 2000.

Urmson, J. O. *Philosophical Analysis*. Oxford: Clarendon Press, 1956.

Whitehead, Alfred North. *Process and Reality: An Essay in Cosmology*. New York: Macmillan, 1929.

Wittgenstein, Ludwig. *Notebooks*. Oxford: Blackwell, 1961.

————. "Some Remarks on Logical Form." *Proceedings of the Aristotelian Society*, supp. vol. 9 (1929): 162–71.

Name Index

Adams, Marilyn McCord, 113n5, 115
Anaxagoras, 77, 90
Anaximander, 90
Aquinas, St. Thomas, 1, 35, 109n3
Aristotle, 1, 6, 17, 50, 75, 97, 104,
    109n2, 109n8, 109n10, 110n2, 112n2
Austin, J. L., 115

Baier, Annette, 111n15, 115
Bain, Alexander, 28, 110n1, 115
Beckmann, Jen P., 109n11, 109n12, 115
Berkeley, George, 77, 90
Bocheński, I. M., 109n8, 115

Carnap Rudolf, 46, 58–59, 90, 111n14,
    115
Celsus, 7
Chaucer, 10
Cicero, 7
Clifford, William Kingdon, 67
Comte, Auguste, 103, 113n6
Copleston, F. S., 111n18

Dancy, R. M., 110n2, 115
Democritus, 53, 90
Descartes, René, 8, 36, 42, 77, 110n3
Dickinson, Jason, 113n7
Dilthey, Wilhelm, 86, 88–90, 110n5,
    112n5, 112n7, 112n9, 115
Diogenes, Laertius, 6
Doyle, Arthur Conan, 109n9, 115

du Bois-Reymond, Emil, 101
Dummett, Michael, 111n22, 115
Duns Scotus, 35, 110n2

Edwards, Paul, 52, 64, 110n3, 115
Empiricus, Sextus, 18
Epicurus, 6
Evans, J. D. G., 112n2

Frege, Gottlob, 36

Gassendi, Pierre, 77
Griffin, D. R., 111n13

Haeckel, Ernest, 101, 102, 115
Hamblin, C. C., 111n5, 115
Hebart, Johann Friedrich, 85, 86
Hegel, G. W. F., 5, 81, 84, 89, 112n3
Hepburn, Ronald W., 111n20, 116
Heraclitus, 77
Hippias, 43
Hobbes, Thomas, 77, 90
Hume, David, 51–52, 64–65, 110n1,
    110n2

James, William, 68, 75, 110n1, 111n21,
    116

Kant, Immanuel, 87, 90, 99–100,
    112n23, 112n6, 113n6, 116
Kekes, John, 112n1, 116

Legendre, A. M. 103, 113n6
Leibniz, G. W., 5, 36, 43, 52, 65, 66, 77, 87, 111n4, 112n23, 116
Leucippus, 54
Lorenz, Kuno, 111n11, 116
Lorenzen, Paul, 56
Lucretius, 6

Marcus, Aurelius, 18
Mill, J. S., 53

Neuarth, Otto, 58, 59

Ockham, William of, 9, 31, 109n11, 116
Omar, Khayyam, 98

Parmenides, 77
Passmore, John, 111n12, 112n11, 116
Pears, D. F., 116
Peirce, Charles Sanders, 2, 3, 46, 103, 111n22, 113n6, 113n10, 116
Perloff, Mickey, 113n7
Plato, 1, 3, 9, 18, 27, 35, 37–38, 79–80, 90, 109n1
Pyrrho, 90
Pythagoras, 77

Quine, W. V. O., 4

Ramsey, Frank P., 39, 110n4, 116
Reichenbach, Hans, 46

Rescher, Nicholas, 109n6, 109n7, 109n8, 110n2, 110n4, 111n13, 112n24, 113n8, 116
Rowe, William L., 111n5, 111n19, 117
Ruetsche, Laura, 113n7
Russell, Bertrand, 5, 55, 56, 58, 64, 109n7, 111n10, 111n18, 117

Schlick, Moritz, 58
Sherbourne, D. W., 111n13
Socrates, 3, 35, 37–38, 80
Spencer, Herbert, 86
Spinoza, Baruch, 4, 36, 42, 77, 78
Stegmüller, Wolfgang, 111n11, 117
Stroll, Avrum, 11n12, 117
Suarez, Francisco, 27

Theophrastus, 6, 109n8

Urmson, J. O., 111n10, 117

Whitehead, A. N., 11, 56–57, 111n13, 117
Wittgenstein, Ludwig, 55–56, 58, 111n6, 111n9, 117

Xanthippe, 35

Zeno, 77, 79